Birgit Fritz

InExActArt

The Autopoietic Theatre of Augusto Boal

A Handbook of Theatre of the Oppressed Practice

Translated by Lana Sendzimir and Ralph Yarrow

For my family, and all those who count me as part of theirs.

Birgit Fritz

InExActArt

The Autopoietic Theatre of Augusto Boal

A Handbook of Theatre of the Oppressed Practice

Translated by Lana Sendzimir and Ralph Yarrow

ibidem-Verlag
Stuttgart

Bibliographic information published by the Deutsche Nationalbibliothek
Die Deutsche Nationalbibliothek lists this publication in the Deutsche Nationalbibliografie;
detailed bibliographic data are available in the Internet at http://dnb.d-nb.de.

Bibliografische Information der Deutschen Nationalbibliothek
Die Deutsche Nationalbibliothek verzeichnet diese Publikation in der Deutschen
Nationalbibliografie; detaillierte bibliografische Daten sind im Internet über http://dnb.d-nb.de
abrufbar.

Translated from the German Original:
Fritz, Birgit: InExActArt - Ein Handbuch zur Praxis des Theaters der Unterdrückten. *ibidem*-Verlag,
Stuttgart 2011. ISBN 978-3-8382-0223-5

ISBN-13: 978-3-8382-0423-9

© *ibidem*-Verlag / *ibidem* Press
Stuttgart, Germany 2012

Printed in the United States of America

Translators' Preface

When Birgit Fritz first told me she was writing a book, she looked like someone who had just discovered that they could fly. It was a beautiful gift to the world that needed to burst out of her, and the excitement was contagious! I was even more touched when she asked me to read the first draft. In a wonderful combination of circumstances, the weekend on which she gave me the manuscript to read, she had also invited me as a guest on a *Theatre of the Oppressed* seminar she was teaching at the university. So in opportune moments and during the breaks I would retreat to a corner to continue reading. It was the ultimate encounter of her work: to read about the history, the ethics and principles, the meaning of this kind of work, its global and political relevance, and then to watch and sense the depth and transformation taking place around and inside of me as the workshop progressed. This is a book to experience, to take and cook with, to challenge and embrace, fall down and get up again, it is work and play, and a journey that goes much further than the last page. For myself, as a younger practitioner gathering experience, it is an invaluable resource to continually return to and be inspired by. Thank you Birgit!

Lana Sendzimir

What struck me most about this book when Birgit asked me to write a Foreword for the German original was its humanity and its wisdom. It speaks in the voice of someone who knows what they are doing because they have been doing it with care, love, precision and understanding. It is more than a book of exercises, it is a book which shares with us the reasons why we might want to do them and teach them to others, and offers us the chance to do them in full awareness of how and why they are working. It's an interactive and dynamic map of how to negotiate the business of becoming more human, which means relating to yourself and to others, becoming what you are and taking the responsibility of acting, in all senses of the word, in consequence.

5

This is a book which needs to be available to the English-speaking community of theatre activists and practitioners, and to those who want to know why theatre activism and practice is useful and timely. It offers clear signposts on the way to helping people to develop the sensitivity, flexibility, alertness and courage to intervene ethically and responsibly in the world. It is both accessible and inspiring. We hope that this translation will help more people make use of it.

Ralph Yarrow

Translators' note

In the German original, whenever appropriate, Birgit Fritz consistently employs grammatical forms which can refer to either gender and thus signals that the persons referred to may belong to either. In English this is unfortunately less easy. We attempt to embrace the principle by using 's/he' and other appropriate pronominal forms; there is no way however to do this with some nouns, except by invoking clumsy terms like 'Jokeress' or 'Spectactress'. The whole text should however, as far as possible, be read in the light of the above principle.

There are several sections which were originally in English, for the most part translated from other languages by other hands or transcribed by Birgit Fritz. We have amended and reworked these where necessary in order to ensure that they fully convey the original writer's or speaker's intentions.

These passages are:

Part B 1: Julian Boal: Notes on Oppression.
Part B 6: Interview with Sanjoy Ganguly. Transcribed by Birgit Fritz
Part D 3: Serando Camara Baldé: Guinean Women. Translated from the Portuguese by Birgit Fritz
Part D 4: Bárbara Santos: *Theatre of the Oppressed in Private Enterprise: Incompatabilities*. Translated from the Portuguese by Carolina Echeverria
Part D 5: Interview with Hector Aristizábal. Transcribed by Birgit Fritz
Appendix 1: The Story of Nebuyenga. Original text provided by Hector Aristizábal
Appendix 2: The Story of the Half-Boy. Original text provided by Hector Aristizábal

'Birgit, you were a real shit the whole time today! And I swear to you I haven't learnt so much in the last seven years in this school as I did today.' Katharina, a pupil in 7th grade at the high school, stood before me.

That year I was teaching Spanish and Performing Arts and we had just experienced a *Forum Theatre* workshop with a visiting trainer, in the course of which I had landed up in the role of the oppressor and my pupils had been playing against me for a whole afternoon.

As Katharina began to speak I began to get nervous and thought: 'Now that doesn't sound like a good start.' Firstly we weren't on familiar terms and then there was the stuff about being a shit. When she'd finished I had goosebumps on my arms.

It was this direct unmediated level of experience which interested me above all.

That day was the beginning of my life with *Theatre of the Oppressed*.

Thanks, Katharina!

Contents

Foreword

We live in a world in which information abounds. We may often wish we could do something to intervene in the situations we hear about. Yet we also often feel powerless: even in 'developed' countries we seem to be suffering from a 'democratic deficit', in spite of political and social systems which claim to afford participation.

At the same time, in recent decades, people across the world have been discovering a way of engaging with their own situation and empowering themselves. *Theatre of the Oppressed* is not an entertainment product but a participatory process which offers people the possibility not simply of receiving information, nor even just of being invited to view different perspectives and possible responses, but of identifying situations and issues, articulating them themselves in the form of short plays, and creating a structure in which an active dialogue between players and spectators is instigated in order to open up further avenues of response. So this is not a passive situation in which a kind of resigned empathy is generated, but an interactive mode of behaviour which stimulates evaluation, critical thinking and imaginative response, and materialises all of this directly for participants by assisting them to embody as well as verbalise the situation, the actors and agents within it, and the potential outcomes.

In the past decade, at least three books (in English) have described the range of practices which can be called 'applied theatre', theatre of the oppressed, theatre of or for development, activist or issue-based theatre, and these build on several decades of work and many reports by practitioners across the globe, not least the pioneering work of Augusto Boal in South America.

This book, written by an experienced practitioner and trainer, offers some glimpses of that work and of the principles underlying it in the form of a short essay by Julian Boal, Augusto's son, on the definition of oppression, and an interview with Sanjoy Ganguly, Artistic Director of the largest and longest-established group working in India, who sees this form of theatre as a politics of relationship leading to a form of practical democracy giving participants a say in shaping their own reality and the contexts in which they live. Its final section also provides examples from practice across the world and shows why and how people are using the processes of theatre to express, assess and respond to the underlying causes of oppression, repression, exclusion and disempowerment, by learning, as Ganguly puts it, to 'script' their own plays and undertake, in Boal's terms, a 'rehearsal of revolution'.

Part 3 contains further developmental strategies for groups: a rich collection of activities to underpin and strengthen individual confidence, group security and mutual understanding, as used by a selection of international practitioners; Part 4 introduces the transcultural dimension of *Theatre of the Oppressed*, exemplifying some instances of its use in Brazil, Germany and elsewhere, and including further reflective essays by practitioners. This section not only gives a picture of some of the ways practitioners work and why they do it, it also opens a window on ongoing debates among the international community of those who engage in this form of theatre, and it foregrounds some challenging questions, in particular about the functioning of all-women groups and the need to interrogate the politics of each and every application across the globe.

However, this is essentially a practical manual, which in the first two sections takes potential trainers and participants through a training method, providing full and clear details of a careful selection of games and exercises which can develop the necessary skills in performers and the necessary techniques for encouraging audiences to play as well. Exercises are throughout set in the context of the aims they are targeting, and this balanced alternation of practice and principle means that it is always possible to see what should be done at each stage of development and why, and also to understand what kinds of response participants may have and how to engage productively with that. Birgit Fritz's experience, sensitivity and clear-sightedness are visible here and make the selection and sequence of exercises accessible and inspiring. So this is a book to use and to live and grow with. Like many of the compilations of theatre games now available (beginning with Keith Johnstone and Clive Barker in the 1960s), this book sets out to suggest and stimulate rather than to require slavish reproduction, and it is by being so clear about purpose that it opens up the space for each user to make the kinds of subtle adaptations which working with different groups in different contexts always demands.

This book will enable you to rationalise what you want to do, and to do it effectively and economically. It takes you through a journey which opens up and sensitises participants – using the 'classic' structure of warm-up, releasing creativity and working together in pairs and small groups to develop interactive response and creative imagination. It then lays out with admirable explicitness precisely how that journey can lead, firstly, to the development of sequences and structures which are key to creating pieces of *Forum Theatre*; and then secondly to the kinds of stimulation, engagement and coaching ('jokering') which invite and enable the direct participation of audience members in proposing and reworking possible alternative outcomes to the problem situations addressed in such plays.

As I write this, another 'Handbook' has just arrived on my desk, also detailing stages and strategies in training and developing a company to do *Forum Theatre*, drawing on experience in western India (this one will be published in English and Gujerati initially). The time is ripe. The world needs practical and cost-effective methods of reconfiguring the lives of individuals and their investment in the structures of society. Here is one way to go about it.

Ralph Yarrow

My Life in the Theatre of the Oppressed

From 1994 to 2000: Teacher for Performing Arts and Languages in a school in Austria

2001: Co-Founder of the *Forum Theatre* Group *Spielerai* for Amnesty International, Vienna

2002: Co-directing *Der Tanz im Narrenturm* (The Dance in the Tower of Fools) with Florian Jung

2002-2004: Theatre trainer for the *Inter>face* Project for the Young Peoples' Intercultural Theatre Group, sponsored by the Vienna Integration Trust

2003: Founder of the Vienna *Theatre of the Oppressed* Organisation *TO Vienna*.

The activity of *TO Vienna* falls into four important phases:

1. Work in collaboration with the Vienna Gebietsbetreuung[1] (2003-2005)
2. Transcultural theatre work with Twin Vision Performance Group (2005-2006)
3. 'Working with Boal' (2006-2008)
4. International networking and multiplication of groups (2006-2011)

In the summer of 2011 TO Vienna passes into other hands and new directions open up.

From 2003: Director of Basic Training in the Theatre Methodology of Augusto Boal in an institute of higher education in Vienna

....
1   Service division of the City of Vienna with responsibility for housing, infrastructure and community life.

From 2004: Visiting Tutor at Vienna University for transcultural theatre, as well as at the Department of African Studies and for the International Development Project; Tutor for integrative theatre work using Boal, in the context of the MA in Latin American Studies and of Peace Studies in Innsbruck, as well as of the Corporate Social Responsibility (CSR) programme for the plenum academy[2], Vienna.

Currently: Freelance theatre-worker, Feldenkrais practitioner and writer.

My work in connection with the *Theatre of the Oppressed* has led beyond Austria to the Basque country, Venezuela, Wales, Portugal, Brazil, the Navajo Nation (USA), India, Croatia, Germany, Slovenia, Kyrgyzstan, and back to my own roots in the dual-language province of Kärnten (Carinthia)/Koroška.

Main emphasis: Transcultural work and research-oriented learning.

---

2   www.plenum.at

Apologetica

In the run-up to the international Jokers' Conference in Rio de Janeiro (2009), Augusto Boal sent out a questionnaire in which all Jokers[3] were asked to record their experiences and usages of *Theatre of the Oppressed*. I counted, and came up with the absurd figure of more than 300 workshops which I had led in the previous ten years.

Absurd, because this figure struck me forcefully and because I found it difficult to reconcile with who I was. To me it seems much more as though there had been only one workshop, always the same one, albeit with different tones, different nuances and in different contexts, with different points of emphasis, but always only one path. *Engeki-Do*, the way of theatre, as my Guatemalan friend Abel Solares, who had lived for many years in Japan, used to say.

Some of these were multiplier programmes[4]; some occurred in the context of theatre projects extending over several years, in which the work rapidly shifted to other levels of theatrical practice, deeper and more lasting. In what way more lasting?

The question of duration is equally absurd when one considers how short my experience with Katharina was and what a change in life-trajectory it generated; even more so since one frequently thinks of duration in connection with long-meditated and deeply considered moves which have been thoroughly prepared and honed. Nothing of this kind had occurred in this case: opting for a life with the *Theatre of the Oppressed* was the work of a moment.

Lasting in the sense of powerful, fascinating, gripping, not letting go, because it touches the Essential.

....
3   The term 'Joker' here may be masculine or feminine. See translators' note at the beginning of the book.
4   To cascade training down by creating more trainers.

Someone once said: 'There's only one meeting in life which is really significant. That's the encounter with someone who knows more than you do, and who is prepared to share this knowledge.'

Meeting with Augusto Boal was like that, and it lives on in his theatre, which fosters encounters. There is a wholeness about this knowledge.

I believe in the magic of Augusto Boal's theatre.

A Handbook for whom?

This book is in four parts. Each part presents a part of investigative theatre praxis in terms of a mode of work and a workshop format which deliver unusual ways of learning. The exercises and activities do not claim to be comprehensive: there are many others like them; nor are they 'perfected' tools, they can be amended; they are also not original in the sense that I lay claim to having discovered them, they were there long before me.

Most of the games come from the 'arsenal' of Boal's *Theatre of the Oppressed*. Others employ processes inspired by Boal but inflected with a particular cultural resonance, i.e. they have often been developed to serve specific needs, like for example the Polarisations of Chen Alon (Israel/Palestine) (see pp. 190-197).

Part 1 looks particularly closely at HOW we interact with each other. It explores the following issues: how consciousness is developed through games and movement, how learning takes place through the body and the senses, how awareness can be increasingly sensitised, how unfamiliar and unusual forms of communication other than speech can be developed, how we can look critically at certain kinds of beliefs and values, how to meet each other with appreciation and respect, and lastly how to work on relating to each other.

The exercises and games can be used by anyone working with diverse groups of people of all ages; they promote the creation of a democratic and dialogic space for learning and produce a sense of solidarity in the group. They reveal analogies of everyday experience and thus create transferable knowledge and recognitions which individuals and groups can apply to whatever contexts they operate in.

The second, central part of the book deals with the practice of *Forum Theatre*, with how it is generated, that is to say how to make issues visible within the group, with the definition of Oppression and with the development of scenes and specific dramaturgical concerns. As a means of intervention in conflict situations, *Forum Theatre* offers the potential of 'communal reflection' about issues which are significant in many contexts across a wide range of societies. People are enabled to become the authors of their own history and to learn how to increase their possibilities of action and their power of imagination. As a means of social transformation, *Forum Theatre* is very flexible; for many theatre activists it is the most important weapon in the arsenal of *Theatre of the Oppressed*.

Julian Boal's essay 'Notes On Oppression' introduces this second part, and the interview with Sanjoy Ganguly about *Forum Theatre* and the ways it can be used in India and Europe rounds off the chapter.

Part 3 provides more extended working methods for relationship work, body awareness and working with objects, as well as *Image Theatre* practice, which is basic to much further work, and some ways of reflecting on the themes of identity, polarisation and the present moment as the starting point of action.

The methods described in this chapter include the *Aesthetics of the Oppressed* and are thus an expression of Augusto Boal's comprehensive conceptualisation of theatre. Theatre as 'the mother of all artistic languages' includes all possible kinds of human expressive forms from painting to musical composition.

The fourth and last part moves beyond the space of the theatre workshop and work on specific themes. It describes the worldwide phenomenon of the *Theatre of the Oppressed* movement and should be read as an attempt to contextualise this liberatory, dialogic method of theatre.

Above and beyond this it is an attempt, drawing on an eclectic selection and examples, to characterise the horizons of some of the elements of theatre practice within which our work occurs.

The examples I have drawn on give an insight into: experimental group work using theatre methodology as a research field and a domain of lived practice; work for and with women as a means of liberation and healing towards what is sometimes called Gaia or Mother Earth; the tension between *Theatre of the Oppressed* and the contemporary economic system, including other forms of didactic theatre; transculturalism as a working principle; peace activism and global politics; and a project report from Guinea-Bissau.

Included here are sections written by the women from Guinea-Bissau, Bárbara Santos and Hector Aristizábal.

Because I am now at the point of writing the Introduction, I know this is a book which will never be finished.

It's up to the reader to fill in the missing pieces, to read further and above all to read back into what has gone before. The books of Augusto Boal and Paulo Freire will fill many of the gaps in this one.

Its aim is to offer people a practical introduction to working with *Theatre of the Oppressed*, whilst at the same time opening up a wider horizon of directions in which one can continue doing practical research if one is interested, using this theatre methodology and the tradition which underpins it.

Along the way you'll have some of the most unexpected and most wonderful experiences and encounters, and life is going to change over and over again in things small and great.

The contact with your own humanity is what also brings out the humanity in others, and you will also become less afraid of what you don't know.

Introduction: The Relationship Shop

The following guiding phrases, rules, laws, comments and working principles should be understood as a background which can support the work in the theatre workshop and help it succeed. They've proved themselves in all kinds of settings and literally in hundreds of workshops and they can be incorporated into the preparation for work, as it were as a kind of 'meditation' for daily practice. They've been collected over many years.

Especially important is a non-judgemental attitude. Emancipatory theatre work operates outside any system of giving marks; that's one of its greatest strengths. When working with others and during regular phases of introspection we can put this into practice. Theatre work is a form of learning by teaching and teaching by learning.

1. Guidelines

If you don't make mistakes you can't learn. We celebrate making mistakes.

Learning for us means: understanding the unknown.

Everyone who comes into the world brings the world a present. The task of the society and the growing child is to find out together what that present consists of, that is, to bring her/his talents and strengths into bloom.

'Don't say what you think, show what you mean!'[5]

Do you have the courage to be happy? And find out what really makes you happy!

....
5   Augusto Boal

Reality consists of movement, sensory awareness, feeling and thinking; that makes what I can experience concrete.

Learning means becoming aware of distinctions. That's called sensitising!

It's not always the best thing to be reasonable. Reasonable stupidity is still stupid.

If too perfect, God's upset![6]

Anxiety keeps us fixated on the same track of action which caused the anxiety in the first place.

Without freedom of choice life is not up to much.

Theatre enables us to relate and hence to experience empowerment and freedom.

Freedom means being part of a collective and being able to feel secure in one's own identity.

Organic learning is lively and enlivening. It happens when you're in a good mood and take frequent short pauses.

One of the foundations of *Theatre of the Oppressed* is recognition of the intelligence of each participant.

The minimum definition of oppression is that oppression rules where monologue has replaced dialogue.[7]

....
6   Car-sticker in California
7   Augusto Boal

According to Paulo Freire, there are teachers who learn and learners who teach.

2. Rules

There are only two important rules.

The first:

Look after yourself. Usually, if everyone obeys this rule, everyone takes care of themselves and of others (this rule includes the proviso that no-one is forced to do anything they don't want to, but at the same time they are seriously invited to take part in an experiment, to try out something new and to be part of a work in progress).

The second:

Never stifle laughter, it's unhealthy![8] If you've got to laugh, laugh; and afterwards concentrate once more on what you're doing.

And one extra rule:

Be aware of the possibility that in this space only things which you want to happen can happen. It's pretty rare to find this in the outside world, but here we have the chance to structure our time in the way that we choose.

---

8   Robin Graham runs laughter workshops in the UK and Africa: see www.writelaugh.co.uk (translators's note).

3. A comment

In order to enter into (a) relationship you need to know and respect your own strengths and weaknesses as well as those of others.

4. A rule

The *Weber-Fechner rule* states that the strength of *subjectively* perceived sense-impressions is proportional to the logarithm of the *objectively* measured intensity of physical stimulus. That means that in order to be aware of distinctions you need to do less. Speed and effort block out information.

You can picture it like this: if we climb a mountain carrying a 40kg rucksack, we won't feel anything when someone places a sandwich on top of the rucksack. If we walk up without a load we will be in a condition to be aware of a small difference in weight.

5. Attitude or the role of heart and mind

In his workshops, Sanjoy Ganguly is fond of telling the story of his friend the psychiatrist. At three in the morning he was woken by the telephone ringing. One of his patients was on the phone, and she told him that she intended to kill herself at the end of the conversation and nothing on earth could stop her. The psychiatrist talked with her, using all his professional skill and knowledge. The conversation went on for two hours, and at the end he was convinced that he could not get through to her and that the next day he would hear of her suicide. The next day he was sitting in his clinic, the door opened and his patient walked in. He was overjoyed and said: 'That's marvellous, I was able to find the right words to help you.' She replied: 'No, doctor. Nothing you said to me was new. I've heard exactly the same arguments from my friends and family over and over again in the last weeks and months.' The psychiatrist was confused and asked: 'Yes, but what stopped you then?' She said: 'It was your attitude. I thought, if someone whom I get out of bed at three in the morning is prepared to spend two hours talking with me, then maybe there is still something in life and it's worth giving it another chance.'

A relationship was established[9]. It was the doctor's attitude to the other person which brought about the change. Lots of theses in books nowadays doubt whether pedagogy can affect human consciousness; maybe it's possible that theatre pedagogy or other relationship work can, so long as it is underpinned by the right attitude and both heart and brain are actively engaged.

6. The working principle: action – reflection – action – reflection

So as to establish a common basis for experience in a group, move back and forth between group activity and group reflection. This alternation of activity and reflection gives the work rhythm.

Since the noise of talking can distract from being aware of sense-impressions, we often work in silence and share our experiences verbally afterwards. We learn more about ourselves and about each other this way.

7. On language

Whichever language we are working in, it's important to speak to all participants, or at least to show that we are trying to do so. In my workshops I always balance gender usage, for example by alternating masculine and feminine forms. Sometimes too I play with language and create completely new forms and expressions.

....
9   A few years later I found the same story in a book by Viktor E. Frankl, who narrates it as having happened to him. Perhaps it's a favourite anecdote with psychiatrists. But that doesn't alter the import.

On this level learned behaviours can be adapted or power structures upheld. That's one component. Another is that if we explore new territory in terms of expressing ourselves, we can begin to think differently too.

Language as a living medium which we use, grows as our consciousness grows, and our consciousness grows as we use language. How we express ourselves reflects the scope of our expressive resources. It isn't a case of trying to be perfect here either, but we can learn to celebrate our mistakes and discover new ones.

If we are a member of a majority group, we need to face up to the challenge when members of minority groups are working with us – whether they are people with special needs[10], people from countries other than our own, or people who are in some way 'other'.

But not only then! Even when we are in groups where everyone is the same, we can practise the reflective use of language. And if now and again we have the experience in life that we are the ones who are 'different', that can also a help extend our sensitivity.

It's fun, it's enlivening.

And if we don't know something or are uncertain about it, then we can ask questions, we can ask for help if we don't know how to say something.

....

10   In my mind I hear the voice of my friend Vera, who does dancing in and out of a wheelchair, saying: 'I don't have any special needs! I want a happy relationship, a good place to work, the same respect that everyone else needs. And unimpeded access to public places. I pay my taxes!' (Did you know that wheelchair dancers call people who dance using their legs 'vertical dancers'? I didn't until recently.)

8. About the games and the methods

The games and exercises presented here are drawn from the 'arsenal' of the *Theatre of the Oppressed*, developed by Augusto Boal in the 1960s and 1970s in Latin America and added to later in Europe.

He taught them for decades throughout the world and so they often have different names. But the best known, like *Columbian Hypnosis, The Vampire of Strasbourg, The Glass Cobra*, are familiar under these names to most Jokers[11].

Many of these games are common property; sometimes they are children's games, or other well-known actor-training games, which Boal collected and published in his book *Games for Actors and Non-Actors*.

Boal, who was proposed for the Nobel Prize in 2008, was in his life (1931-2009) an ambassador for human rights, dialogue and transculturalism. His attitude was that all people are capable of solving their problems, acting to bring about a better world and shaping this according to their own ideas, since they know best how to improve their own circumstances. This respect for and belief in people is what distinguishes Augusto Boal's work most profoundly.

Boal, who was in the 50s and 60s a well-known avant-garde Latin-American director, learnt from Paulo Freire to make his theatre accessible to all, even those who normally have nothing to do with theatre at all.

He called theatre 'the mother of all arts' because it includes language (as text), tonality (as music) and visual forms (as images). His understanding of theatre is very broad, it is a 'theatre for everyone', and everything which is found in life has a place in it, even if that means we maybe wouldn't call it theatre any more.

....
11   See Part B Point 6

Boalian theatre, whatever name it is given, is currently used in over 80 countries and on every continent; and as it travels around the world it changes and grows, new games and new ways of using them are added, new rules are invented. What never changes is the importance of human rights, and of the ethical and philosophical principles which underlie them, in this work.

Every year there are festivals and workshops in Africa (especially in Senegal, in Burkina Faso, in Mozambique, Guinea-Bissau and Angola), in Asia (India, Kolkata), but also in Europe (in Croatia, Austria, Spain, France, Sweden etc.) and in Latin America.

When we play these games then, we are part of a very large and numerous community of people who use this theatre and its methods and games to improve their lives and to discover things about life and about themselves. It is theatre as a form of research and it makes us members of a worldwide theatre movement to humanise humanity[12].

The theatre work of Augusto Boal is a 'discipline' which has grown organically and is rooted in history; essentially then it is a way of engaging with and applying theatre as an emancipatory, participatory and dialogic practice which is committed to the development and transformation of society.

It arose at a particular moment in history from a specific political situation and it has changed and grown over the years in response to conditions in those regions in which it has been applied.

This means that these exercises, methods and games are indeed games, but they have a serious purpose and they are not intended to be used indiscriminately or simply for amusement.

....
12   See Declaration of Principles of the *Theatre of the Oppressed*, Appendix 3

It is the intention behind the methods which shapes what they produce, namely the *Theatre of the Oppressed*, as Augusto Boal writes in his book *The Aesthetics of the Oppressed*[13]:

'The *Theatre of the Oppressed* is an ethical theatre, [a theatre in which] nothing can be done unless we know why and for whom it is being done. [...] The ethical significance of every action is as important as the action itself.'

So it is theatre with and for a purpose.

Further information can be found at www.theatreoftheoppressed.org, www.ptoweb.org and many other sites. Books by and about Augusto Boal and Paulo Freire are listed in the Bibliography.

Commentary on the *Tree of the Theatre of the Oppressed* (see figure 1):

The methods of *Image Theatre*, *Forum Theatre* and *Newspaper Theatre* were developed in Latin America (Brazil, Peru and Argentina) prior to Augusto Boal's exile. During his exile in Europe he, along with his wife Cecilia Thumin-Boal, developed the techniques of the *Rainbow of Desire*[14]. After his return to Brazil, *Legislative Theatre* and the summative volume *The Aesthetics of the Oppressed*[15] were published.

This book confines itself to the 'basic vocabulary' of the arsenal of *Theatre of the Oppressed*, in other words to the sections and aspects of the method which I draw on most frequently in my work.[16] Boal's book *Legislative Theatre*

---

13 Boal, Augusto, *The Aesthetics of the Oppressed*, Routledge, London 2006, p. 50
14 They may also have drawn on other work: for example, forms of 'Living Newspaper' appear in Jakob Moreno's *Stegreiftheater* in Vienna, in Chicago 'improv' and in Turkish *orta oyunu* (see Frost, Anthony & Yarrow, Ralph, *Improvisation in Drama*, Palgrave, London 2007 (translators' note)).
15 N.B. The English version (2006) differs significantly from the later Portuguese edition (2009) cited in the Bibliography.
16 Further information about *Newspaper Theatre* can be found in Boal's books. See Bibliography.

describes this experiment in detail and serves as an inspiration to go on look-ing for new contemporary ways for people to intervene in political life.

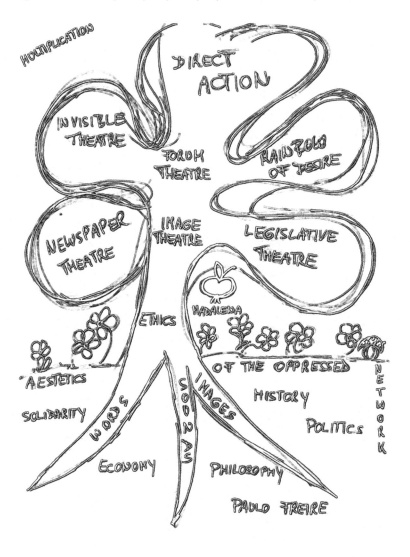

Figure 1 The *Tree of the Theatre of the Oppressed*

The largest *Legislative Theatre* project in Europe that I know of at the time of writing was co-ordinated by Iwan Brioc in Wales (*The Agora Project*). (Theatr Fforwm Cymru, 2002)

And for the first time since the 1990s, when Augusto Boal linked *Theatre of the Oppressed* and executive politics directly as an elected representative in Rio de Janeiro, José Soeiro in Portugal is following suit as the youngest European member of Parliament who is also a representative of the *Theatre of the Oppressed*[17] community.

The methods of *Rainbow of Desire* work often crop up in our work, but in order to provide a more straightforward way in and to avoid making the dish too rich I have refrained from dealing with them in this book.

The two best-known stories (or parables) in TO, 'The story of Virgílio' and 'The story of the fat lady', which describe key turning points in Boal's life and in the development of TO, can be found in an Appendix: they are told in almost every workshop.

9. On learning and leading

Learning is made up of thinking, sense-impressions, feeling and doing.

People learn best when not under stress, in a relaxed, alert condition. Getting things wrong is part of learning, it's natural.

When setting up learning spaces we should try to make them as agreeable as possible, free of particular connotations and arranged so that everyone can be involved. That means that the life-situation of the participants should be taken into account, any individual needs respected (e.g. access, translation if neces-

....

17   In English the abbreviation 'TO' is usual for *Theatre of the Oppressed*. GTO stands for 'Group of *Theatre of the Oppressed*' and CTO for 'Centre of the *Theatre of the Oppressed*'.

sary) and there must be no compulsion. At the same time there needs to be agreement about the requirements of the work, so that some framework is established.

All transactions should be clearly structured; content should take precedence over form. Time should not be used as a means of manipulating action or outcomes.

In spite of all this, there is a role for leadership. That is to look after the framework, to make it possible to work with the methods, to be aware at all times of the process of the work and to support it; but the protagonists of what is happening are the participants, and leadership should remain attentively and productively in the background. But that's a very good place to be!

A. Building Relationships

Figure 2 International Workshop Jana Sanskriti 2010

Figure 3 International Workshop Jana Sanskriti 2010

Figure 4 International Workshop Jana Sanskriti 2010

Games and exercises to develop awareness within the group and within individuals, and to sharpen the leader's awareness of the group.

Themes Part A

Introduction to ways of working, overcoming habitual and mechanical behaviour, achieving stillness, focusing, attention, care for self and others, seeing and being seen, reducing sensory input in order to allow others to become more visible, recognising and respecting boundaries, trust – above all in oneself; but here it's also true to say that a certain amount of bewilderment is not harmful to the learning process (but don't worry, there's no need to try to build this in, it will happen anyway).

These games are not 'only' games. First and foremost they are a form of 'learned and experienced life'. Movement, contact, laughter, liveliness and the recovery of trust in one's own spontaneity are kinds of information which 'inform' more than just the moment of their occurrence: like all everyday activities, they inscribe themselves on body and mind and extend our repertoire of action and movement.

But more than this. By awakening our dormant talents and qualities, we can unlock our creative resources and thus become more resilient, more free and autonomous in confronting our daily challenges. What we call the *spirit of playfulness*[18] helps us to react more spontaneously and less dutifully to situations, and our claims to perfection recede into the background. Pleasure in the now, in the experience of the moment, is allowed more space.

Respectful and reflective physical contact allows us to encounter our traumas in a playful way and to juxtapose new experiences alongside them. This is particularly important in a culture which veers between excess and prudishness

....
18   cf. Schiller's *Spieltrieb* (play-drive) perhaps (translators' note).

(life in consumer society, voyeuristic spectacle such as reality shows, the sexualisation of public space through advertising, burn-out in the workplace and so on) and has lost its bearings in terms of negotiating human contact. To a certain extent our range of language and expression has been truncated. We experience ourselves as impoverished.

As things which we thought were ours by right have become taboo or problematic, others, which would otherwise have deserved closer attention (do we have enough free time? breaks at work? how is our health situation?) also tend to slip out of focus.

In a theatre workshop, which makes available a voyage within as well as a journey into society, we get the chance to use these possibilities of expression to answer sensory, emotional and also intellectual questions, or at least to start the search for answers.

If we make this clear to participants at the outset, we can alert them to the possibility of keeping a theatre or workshop diary and recording their internal and external experiences and 'movements'. There may be space to share whatever people wish to share with others in the group in periods of reflection. It's good to point out that it is completely in order for people to keep things to themselves as well. Voluntary participation is always desirable. Sometimes we work in contexts where things are different. There are some reflections about this in the texts in Part D of this book.

The games and exercises described below are all classics. For those who are interested, I have described what kinds of 'information' groups or individuals can take from the experience at the end of each exercise. It's not necessarily the case that this will be recognised by all individuals, but nevertheless this information is part of what emerges from the process.

For all these exercises the following applies: They should be introduced as simply and briefly as possible, so as not to preclude direct experience for each player. If players alter the rules creatively, or interpret them individually, that's fine, so long as no-one is in any way endangered by this. It is important that the period of exchange and reflection which follows practice should be dialogic in nature, and that everyone's voice can be heard.

1. Starting Point

When I begin to work with a new group, the first few minutes are always the most apprehensive. No one really knows what to expect, everyone is still in their own head-space, and the first task is to create a new, collective space of experience. Movement is the best way to do this is.

Depending on the context, there is usually always time, after a half an hour of activity, to exchange important organisational and theoretical information.

To begin with it is good to 'walk' the room. This can be accompanied by the following:

'Walk about in the room and continually change direction. Watch out that you do not bump into anyone, and take up as much space as possible. How are the soles of your feet making contact with the floor? Relax your shoulders, let your arms hang by your sides. Relax your eyebrows. Often we carry unconscious stress in our eyebrows. So walk as though you know where you are going. Relax your lower jaw, and make your face soft like butter.'

And then continue with the following exercise:

People 2 people

Figure 5 Workshop in Kyrgyzstan 2007

Let's walk around in the room, and at the sound of a clap, we will...

- shake as many hands as possible and then continue walking
  At the next clap:
- greet each other in as many languages and in as many different ways as possible
- with your right knee softly touch as many other right knees as possible
- do the same with the left shoulder
- or ear to ear
  Stand together with those people who:
- come from a village, or from a town
- are born in the same month
- have the same eye colour, sock colour, etc.
- have had a vacation in the South, etc.

Supplementary Note

Spatial orientation; first touch, gentle, without bruises; doing something unfamiliar; encountering many new people, or else encountering familiar people in unfamiliar ways. Enhancing bodily consciousness; touching unfamiliar parts (ear). What we are doing here is simple and everyone can take part in it – don't be scared!

Variation

Now, walk about in the room. When you hear the group leader clap, stop, balance on one leg, hold each other's hands, legs raised in the air touching, stretch and smile!

This instruction almost always needs to be repeated a second time, and once it's been done, the further instruction 'don't forget to breathe!' is useful.

Because this exercise produces very nice group images, it can be repeated two or three times. At the end we applaud ourselves!

Supplementary Note:

This way we create our first image and are able to 'lean out' further than on our own, we give each other support, we are connected, held by a web.

1 2 3 – Bradford – counting to three – with a partner[19]

Choose a partner for this next essential game in our relationship toolbox.

In pairs, count to three. Person A says: 'One', Person B says: 'Two', Person A says: 'Three' and then it starts over. If this works, we can make it a bit more difficult: we replace number One with a movement and a sound, which should be made by a vocal sound. For example: wiggling your hands and saying 'Tschaboom'.

These movements and sounds replace saying 'One', the rest stays the same (A and B continue to alternate 'Tschaboom' plus movement, 'Two, Three'), meaning both partners make the same movement and sound instead of saying 'One'. If doing this goes well, then the number Two is also replaced with a second movement and sound, and later the number Three, until all are replaced.

We have found a new form of expression!

Variation or extension:

The result is three different movements and sounds, now try to do them as quietly as possible, i.e. without sound. Next, try to do this with closed eyes.

Afterwards we can show each other our 'choreographies': half of the room shows the other half, and then the other way around.

....
19   Exercises in pairs provide the opportunity to work with different people as often as possible, until we know everyone in the group.

Supplementary Note:

We all possess creativity, a voice, and movement. We can carry out a task despite our leaving behind the 'normal' interaction patterns we have with one another. Seeing and being seen! And we can be both loud and quiet, and listen intuitively. And if we make mistakes that's also fine. Together we have also abandoned our 'normal' behaviour and entered a new realm of experience. There will – surely – be laughter!

Walk! Stand still! Say your name! Jump!

Everyone walks around in the room. When the group leader says 'Walk!', then everyone must stand still. When he or she says: 'Stand still!', then everyone walks. Then two further prompts are added: when the group leader says 'Name!', everyone says their name and continues doing what they had been doing beforehand (walking or standing). When the prompt to 'Jump!' comes, then everyone jumps. So 'Walk!' means 'Stand still!', 'Stand still!' means 'Walk!', 'Say your name!' means 'Say your name!', and 'Jump!' means 'Jump!' Then the meaning of the latter two are also switched around.

To make it more difficult the group leader can also do the opposite of what he or she says. Further suggestions can also come from the leader or from the group itself (such as: when prompted 'Head!', everyone taps their head, and with 'Bottom!', they tap their bottom, etc.).

In the end the meanings are:

$$\begin{aligned}
\text{Walk!} &= \text{Stand still!} \\
\text{Stand still!} &= \text{Walk!} \\
\text{Say your name!} &= \text{Jump!} \\
\text{Jump!} &= \text{Say your name!}
\end{aligned}$$

The same goes for suggestions from the group.

Supplementary Note:

Challenges are fun! Making mistakes are too!

Excursus: The Small-Group Reflection

The reflections are always determined by the aims of our work, as well as by the time and resources at our disposal. Naturally, the type of language and complexity these reflections carry, depends upon the participants. The more diverse the group, the richer the content they have to share and the more intensively they can use the time.

In my workshops, which often last between two and twelve days, and frequently have a trans-cultural focus, the reflections shared at the beginning are particularly important to me in order to make differences apparent and to thus awaken the sensitivity towards diversity.

The easy accessibility of this work creates space for self-observation and the experience of subtle things, which are often imperceptible in the reality of the outside world. Sharing what I feel makes it clear that I'm not exceptional but part of a community of people fundamentally identified by their needs, concerns, likes and sensitivities. To sense this is exciting and important.

The ability to be empathetic begins with the recognition of our own needs. A participant in one of my recent workshops told me: 'When you say NO you say Yes to yourself!' Respecting yourself leads to respect for the behaviour and idiosyncrasies of others. What this really means: the ability to be as you are, take breaks when you need them, and sometimes skip an exercise.

Depending on the group's size, I propose an exchange of experiences in smaller groups, and then ask them to share the most important things when we all come together again. The number of opportunities for reflection I integrate throughout the day depends on the make-up of the workshop and its focus as a whole.

When reflecting together with the whole group, it's a good idea to wait patiently until someone begins to speak. Our inability to wait has become a malaise of our time. The experiences they have had continue to 'work' within each person and it might take time before these can be put into words. A theatre teacher who was important to me once said: 'You have to listen to the silences. You never know what they will bring.' Remembering this has often proved itself very useful.

Sample questions[20]

'How are you feeling?', 'How did you get here?', 'How are you doing now?', 'What struck you while you were here?', 'What did you like, what didn't you?', 'What did you experience?', 'How do I deal with situations in which I feel disoriented?', 'What were the experiences of communicating without language like for you?', 'What worked well and what less well?', 'Which contradictions were interesting for you?'

....
20 Many of the questions here are suggested for grade school use. When working with other groups the reflection round can of course be left more open, or rather, have other focal points; or just have a break.

2. Sensitisation Games

Theatre is relationship! When we wish to enter into a relationship with one another, it is important to be aware of our own strength, as well as our partner's. Because when we play out our strengths, or our superiority over someone else, in order to 'out-act' the other person, it is probably the most boring thing we could do. It is far more exciting to discover our diverse range of talents and to see what we can create with them together. We should also get a sense of weaknesses and constraints, both our own and others'. Only then can we be mindful of them and take care of each other.

The following game is about strength, how it feels when we renounce it, and which forces act upon us of their own accord.

Capoeira – exercise for pairs

Capoeira is a martial art form, long disguised as dance, which developed in Brazil during the time of slavery. The focus is on maintaining balance and speed, but also on shared play.

This is a rather slow and thus more challenging exercise.

Find a partner who is roughly the same height as you are. Stand facing one another, such that your bent forearms are able to touch. The rules are, that your forearms must never lose contact with each other, and no physical force may be used. The aim of the game is to gently touch your partner's face with your fingers, while preventing him or her from touching yours.

This requires a lot of movement in the spine, because running away is not an option!

Do this for three minutes with your partner, and then for one minute with one or two different people. Everyone develops their own strategy, try to feel and compare the differences! Your muscles should be used as little as possible, but don't lose sight of your goal! Cooperation and agility without force are necessary.

Afterwards, sit together with your partner on the floor, discuss the exercise and how it felt for both of you.

If there is time, you may also relate your experiences in the larger group.

Supplementary Note:

Acting in opposition, pursuing a goal, but also maintaining the sense of shared play, achieving your goal without using physical force, sensing your partner's resistances, allowing prolonged contact, slowing down the movement allows more information and more contact. Experiencing differing strategies from different partners, as well as our own reactions to them. Accepting the slowness of the encounter.

Gravity – exercise for pairs

The force of gravity is unlike muscle power, it's more like renouncing muscle power. Without any effort on our part, gravity is constantly acting upon us. We can play with this.

We can hold each other's hands, bend our knees, sit down simultaneously and then stand up again. Or, one person stands, the other one bends his/her knees and rocks backwards and forwards. The same exercise can be done with three people, with four, or even in a small circle.

It's important that partners should hold each other's wrists, not simply grip with their fingers (slippery).

Variation

Stand back to back; maintain as much contact between yourself and your partner as possible (from pelvis to shoulders). From this position, without holding hands, try to sit down together. If it works, repeat it.

We can allow ourselves to be held, give and take weight, create a counterbalance, take or pass on responsibility. Be aware of the body and make it available as part of a shared interaction.

3. Trust Exercises

Trust exercises are not meant to be used to manipulate the group dynamic, they are a way in which to encounter our sensitivity, as well as our own limits, and thus reorient ourselves. This takes place in a caring environment and has nothing to do with sensationalism. More often than not during this exercise, more takes place inside people than outside. Frequently, exercises that challenge us appear harmless and unspectacular on the outside. These last two belong in this category.

In the following two exercises, it is important that the person in the middle feels comfortable. This usually works best when no there is no talking, and when everything is done very slowly.

Joe Egg

Form several small circles of at least six people, with one volunteer standing in the middle.

To begin with, we place our hands on the person in the middle, letting their body know that we are really THERE. Our body has its own 'head'. When we feel, we know more than when we believe.

The person in the middle, with their eyes closed, is then slowly 'passed around' within the circle. While doing this, make sure that no one takes on more weight than they are able to carry, and that the person in the middle is touched respectfully and gently. Less is more! One person should be 'held' by at least two others. And there should be enough time for everybody to have a turn in the middle. It is helpful for the person in the middle to stand straight and firm, like a tree trunk, so that they do not bend! If they prefer, they can also cross their arms over their chest in protection, which can also make it easier for others to give them support.

Flying

A volunteer lies down on the floor face up. At least seven others slowly carry him/her on a walk around the space. There should be at least three people on each side and a person solely responsible for carrying the head. We lift the person as high as we are able to manage, and the person being carried feels comfortable with. The walk can be shorter or longer, depending on our strength and time.

It's important to lower the person to the floor slowly, which is the most pleasant part of the exercise.

Variation

The King/Queen

The King/Queen is never allowed to touch the floor, but can go wherever they wish to go. The group's task is to act as 'floor' and 'props' for them. Kings/Queens can thus move 'through the air' above the shoulders of the others.

Supplementary Note:

Working in silence and with concentration, with the goal of enabling each other to have unusual, pleasant experiences. Opening yourself up to adventures, being carried, feeling held: the feeling of timelessness in the workshop. The offer should only be made if there is really enough time for the exercise, such that each person who would like to can experience it: space for self-awareness, without rushing.

Afterwards, or during a longer break, it is good to have the opportunity to share experiences.

Figure 6 *TO Vienna*, Workshop with Maria Nora from Living Theatre Cologne

The best-known exercise of the *Theatre of the Oppressed*:

Colombian Hypnosis[21] – exercise for pairs

One of the most central games in *Theatre of the Oppressed* work is called Columbian Hypnosis. In it, the face of one partner and the hand of the other are magnets, and the distance between them must always remain the same. One partner thus leads the other with the palm of their hand. After five to ten minutes the roles are then switched.

---

21 Google *Colombian Hypnosis* online. You will find many pictures of people from all over the world, doing this exercise.

Figure 7 International Workshop Jana Sanskriti 2010

Figure 8 *TO Vienna*, Workshop with Sanjoy Ganguly 2007

While doing this exercise it is important to be aware and take care of the physical and psychological abilities of your partner (don't make anyone dizzy!), otherwise they may reject the game and leave you without a partner. After five minutes the roles can then be switched. So be careful! 'Revenge' is coming.

One aim of this exercise is to help your partner to move in ways they may not have thought of on their own. This can make them aware of forgotten and unexpected possibilities, and encourages mobility.

There are many ways in which this game can be varied, such as:

- leading more than one person simultaneously (e.g. with each hand, and with your knees as well)
- leading while being led. What can we experience by doing it this way?
- inspiring movement in your partner's whole body by moving your hand and fingers in particular ways (e.g. like a jellyfish, making them bigger or smaller, quick finger movements etc.
- using sounds to comment on these movement qualities

Tip: The exercises change a lot depending on how much time they are given to 'unfold'. The players enter a different state of perception when they sense that the games are not some form of 'occupational therapy', but genuine realms of experience and reflection. Try it out!

Furthermore, you can sense when observing them, whether participants are still interested in the activity. So, calmly observe and trust your feeling.

A really nice thing I learned from Julian Boal, is to announce the ending of an exercise. When I have the feeling that enough time has been spent on an exercise, I say: 'One more minute!' Then everyone knows that the 'weird business' is coming to an end, and time is being taken care of. But they also have time to try the exercise one last time and explore it before it is ended abruptly. How long that 'felt' minute lasts, well, that's another story!

Supplementary Note:

The game can be seen as a metaphor for the handling of power and discussed in that light. It is a good opportunity to reflect upon the role of leader and of being led. Question: 'What did you like best?', 'Why?', 'What is relaxing?', 'What is challenging?', 'How do you feel about power?', 'Is it always there?', 'Who has it?', 'When do we lose it?', 'How can we share it?'

Tip: The exercise can also be used to find images of conflict and oppressive situations, for the development of *Forum Theatre* scenes. This is done by 'freezing'[22] the action at regular intervals, to see which scenarios have arisen. If you find a few that seem interesting, they can be presented to the group for interpretation.

....
22 'Freeze' means: when you hear 'Stop!' stand still in that particular shape, as though frozen.

4. Exercises with closed eyes

Figure 9 International Workshop Jana Sanskriti 2010

The various exercises in the *Theatre of the Oppressed* repertoire can be divided into the following categories:

> Feel what you touch!
> Listen to what you hear!
> See what you look at!

Overall they serve to dynamise, to enliven conscious awareness of the senses, stimulate awakening of body-memory and the holistic functioning of human thinking and feeling.

Some games and exercises edit out perception through one channel of the senses in order to stimulate those remaining to heightened activity and enhanced recognition.

Feel what you touch – exercise for pairs

The most well-known exercise practised with eyes closed in the TO repertoire: one partner leads the other (who keeps his/her eyes closed) through the environment. In doing so, the person with opened eyes leads the hand of their non-seeing partner to various objects, things, plants, cloth etc. The 'curious' hand can decide for itself how long it would like to explore something, and when it's had enough. Then the seeing partner leads him/her to a different place.

The aim of this exercise is to experience the familiar in new, unfamiliar ways. It's not a guessing game, but a process of 'reading' using fingers and hands. After roughly ten minutes the partners switch roles, but of course this exercise can be done for a much longer period of time, especially if you are outside in nature. A one hour walk becomes nothing, the time flies by.

When both partners have undergone the experience, they talk about what they got from it, first as a pair and subsequently with the entire group.

Supplementary Note:

When we close our eyes, we begin to respond to things in a more sensitive way: the uneven floor, temperature differences, light and dark, the surface texture of things we touch, whether they are animate or not, sounds etc. The way our feet touch the floor and pass on information concerning our balance, will be experienced more intensely. Connecting to past memories, new images appear, and questions emerge.

121212 or Penguin Family – a favourite game!

Stand in a circle. You will need an even number of participants to play this game. Count round the circle alternately: one, two, one, two, one, two, until each person has a number, either a one or two. Then it can begin:

First, all the Ones stand in front of the Two on their right-hand side. They look each other in the face. Then the Twos close their eyes. The Ones make a sound, which they can maintain for a long time and by which the Twos will be able to recognise them. Meanwhile the game leader moves around to make sure that there are no identical sounds that might be confused. The Ones then move back to their original position in the circle, and the Twos can open their eyes again.

Now the Twos step out to stand in front of the One to their right-hand side. They are now in front of a different person! The Ones then close their eyes and the Twos make a new sound, by which the Ones will later be able to recognise them. The Twos then also return to their place in the circle.

Next, everyone in the circle closes their eyes, and begins to imagine that they are penguins, mamas and papas and penguin babies. Silently, all of them then begin to slowly and carefully toddle through the space. When they hear the words: 'reconstruct the circle!', 'find your neighbour!', everyone begins to make their sound, to find their neighbours, their penguin family again.

When they have found them, they hold hands and stop making their sounds. Those who are still searching continue making their sound until the circle is completed and everyone is holding hands.

The Vampire of Strasbourg

With their eyes closed, the entire group moves carefully through the space. For more safety, you can hold your bent arms in front of you at chest height. There is no vampire in the room yet! As soon as the leader chooses someone, by touching them on their shoulder, they become the vampire!

The vampire can then, as soon as they touch someone else (as in the Capoeira game, running away is not possible, especially with closed eyes!), gently, with both hands, 'bite' them in the shoulder. This of course – only figuratively – hurts dreadfully and causes loud cries of pain. The person who has been bitten is then also transformed into a vampire by the bite, such that the number of vampires increases as the game continues.

When there are several vampires in the room, it's possible that one vampire may bite another. For the vampire being bitten, this is a very pleasant experience, accompanied by loud noises of enjoyment – making him or her human once more.

For many, having the courage to awaken the voice and really enjoy it, can be a more striking experience than we on 'the outside' might expect.

Excursus: Who am I? Name and concentration game for the beginning or during the workshop.

Name games are plentiful, and for many of us they bring up unpleasant sensations, because they remind us of a time when we were perhaps unable to remember the names of people in the group. It's best to begin playfully, by degrees, and be open about not being able to remember all the names at once, especially in a large group.

In terms of other, more personal information, my experience has taught me not to ask personal questions. All too often, these remind us of public, official routines ('Who are you?', 'Where do you come from?', 'Where is your family?', 'Why are you here?', 'What is your job?', 'What, you don't have a job?', 'How much money do you have in the bank?', 'None?') and pigeon-holing, which we don't want to reproduce in this context. Over the course of the time we spend together we will share what we are happy to share, and perhaps we will learn things that we would not have learned if we asked directly.

5. Name Games

Name/No Name

This is a name game after which no-one knows each person's name, but knows all the names: all the players find a spot in the space, so that everyone is spread out evenly.

Step 1

The participants close their eyes as the leader moves around amongst them. When s/he touches someone on the shoulder, that person calls out their name.

Step 2

After a short pause, all the participants again close their eyes (or rather, they remain closed) and the leader runs about amongst them again. When s/he touches a participant this time, the person calls out the name they just heard beforehand.

When everyone opens their eyes again, they have heard all the names, but do not necessarily know to whom they belong: the universe has got the information!

Ball Throwing

We stand in a circle and throw a ball to a person with whom we have made eye contact. While we throw it, we say our own name. We can do so with several balls at the same time.

In the second round, we throw the ball and say the name of the person to whom we are throwing.

Name and Image

Step 1

Everyone stands in a circle. One person begins: s/he steps into the circle, takes a physical shape, expressing him/her self at that moment, and saying his/her own name. The whole group then repeats the shape and name together.

Step 2

Once all gestures, or shapes, have been shown, you can 'call' someone whose name and shape you have remembered by repeating it. This person then steps into the circle, having 'heard' you, repeats his/her shape and name, and then does a different one 'belonging' to another person, calling on them.

In this second round you can sometimes skip saying the name.

Name and Image – exercise for pairs

Two people introduce themselves to each other by describing some things about themselves that they feel happy to share. First one person speaks, then the other. While the first person speaks, the other person draws a picture of him/her, or rather, an interpretation of their partner's words: drawing, BUT without looking at the piece of paper. Then the partners switch roles. Subsequently, each pair introduces itself to the entire group, and presents their partner's picture, recounting what information they can remember from what their partner told.

Variation

During the presentation, the partners can stand behind one another. The person in front speaks, while the one behind reaches through, underneath the arms of the person in front, and becomes his/her arms. From here s/he can take over the gesticulation, and possibly amend it with any different understandings s/he may have had of what her/his partner recalls.

Name and Vegetable

A name game in which all the group members will learn everybody else's name:

The group stands in a circle and one person begins. They say their name prefaced by the name of a vegetable whose name begins with the same letter as their own name. The next person repeats what the person before them has said, and adds the name of a vegetable beginning with the first letter of their own name, as well as their own name. Each subsequent person in the circle must repeat all the names and vegetable names preceding them before they can add their own vegetable and name (e.g. Marjoram Magda, Fennel Frankie,

Artichoke Andrea etc.). Finally, the first person must repeat the entire vegetable- and name-chain.

Variation

The same game, but using adjectives starting with the same letter as the person's name does.

Name Whisper – exercise for pairs

This is a very quiet name game, after which everyone knows the name of at least one other person. In it, one person leads another around in the space, in between all the other people, whilst whispering his/her partner's name. All the pairs do this simultaneously.

The game requires concentration and careful awareness (one must make sure not to run into people behind us as we lead). The more quietly it is played, the better. After five to ten minutes the roles are swopped without speaking.

As a follow-up, pairs can first reflect amongst themselves, and later with the entire group. Consider how the game felt for you, how it may have altered your spatial awareness and your perceptions in general[23].

The role of the leader is also a 'name', having a certain position within the group, as explored in the following game.

....
23   Scientific findings on this can be found online using the phrase 'Cocktail party Effect'.

Leader and Liar – Who's lying here?

Figure 10 Julian Boal during the festival in Pula 2010 – He brought us this game

The participants form two circles of equal size, and the leader explains the rules of the game: Everyone will close their eyes and wait. Then the leader will run around the circles and touch one person in each circle on the shoulder. This person will become the leader, but must not under any circumstances reveal this. Once a person has been chosen in both circles, everyone may open their eyes again, and must find out who the leader is without talking, only through feeling. They must collectively agree on one person (who will naturally point to a different person) and point to them. No-one should speak. The group must remember the person identified as the leader in the first round, and then there is a second round of the same sequence. Again, the group must unanimously identify one person as the leader.

Afterwards, the group remains silent and sits down together. They can then begin talking, but to begin with they only discuss the ways in which we discern whether someone is lying. When the discussion is finished, the leader of the exercise asks all of the 'leaders' chosen during the game's first round to raise their hands. The result: everyone raises their hand. Then s/he asks the 'leaders' chosen in the second round to raise their hands. The result: no one raises their hand.[24]

During the subsequent discussion (on questions like: 'How can you tell if someone is lying?', 'How can you make decisions in a group?', 'How can you divert attention away from yourself?') about cultural, or alternatively, individual forms of expression for 'innocent', 'respectful', 'polite' behaviour, it becomes clear that we are probably not likely to judge the behaviour of others in certain situations. The lying leader of the exercise was raised above suspicion by his/her status in the group.

In Austrian history of the last ten years, the judgement of gesture and facial expression, particularly during court trials of Austrian residents from different countries of origin, has been a frequent issue.

Concentration Circle: Favourite foods, Car brands and YOU!

Everyone stands in a circle and one person tells another person what his/her favourite food is. This other person in turn names their own favourite food to the next person in the circle. This continues until every person in the circle has named their favourite kind of food, and ends up back at the first person. Then the same sequence is done again, with the same foods and the same order, repeating it several times for practice.

When everyone is able to do this, a new round is started, with a new sequence, this time with car brands. When this sequence has also been practised several times, both sequences (food and cars) can be run through at the same

---

24 In the first round everybody's shoulder was touched, in the second nobody's was.

time. It is important to remember who you say something to and who says something to you.

Variation

If the first version goes well, you can add a further element whereby, if someone points to another person and says 'You!', these two people must switch places. Once they have taken their new places in the circle, then the 'You!' is also passed on, but this time in no specific order. For this to work, a high level of concentration is necessary from everyone! This is a very good 'Theatre Sports' game, particularly when working with groups of young people and before performances.

6. Action Games, to make people laugh and take away the fear of making 'mistakes'

We live in a predominantly judgemental, fear-promoting society. In the theatrical, playful, exploratory space, this attitude, which confronts us all too often in our lives, can be defused: laughing heals!

Moreover, it is also true that we experience our abilities – particularly the simplest ones – very little in our daily lives. By this I mean things like laughing, dancing, jumping, singing, being silent, pausing and letting our weight be held by the ground.

Godzilla, or 'Can I please take your place?'

Everyone finds a partner, hooks arms with them; then all the pairs form a circle. A volunteer goes into the middle. The person in the middle must move clockwise around the circle while asking 'Can I please take your place?' or 'Can I please have your partner?' The others may answer with 'No' – in which case the person must move on – or with 'Yes' – then they swop places.

The players in the circle can switch places when the person asking for a spot isn't looking, communicating with winks, so that the person in the middle cannot find a free space. If s/he finds a free spot, then a new person is left in the middle of the circle.

After a while someone can shout 'Godzilla!' This is the cue for everyone to begin running about in the room. To get to safety, they must find a new partner. Once two people have found each other, they must embrace each other in slow motion, with exaggerated emotion, like in a bad Hollywood movie. The person left over, unable to find a partner, is the new questioner in the centre of the circle.

Rain, House, Person

Figure 11 International Workshop Jana Sanskriti 2010

Figure 12 International Workshop Jana Sanskriti 2010

For this game you will need several groups of three and yourself! Each group of three builds a house; two people for the roof, standing with raised arms and touching palms, the third person sits beneath them in the house. One person stands in the midst of these houses. If she/he calls out 'House!', then all the houses change places and find a new partner (who had been part of a house before) to create a new roof over one of the sitting people. If the person in the middle calls out 'Person!', then all the people sitting in a house must swop places. If the person says 'Rain!', then everyone must switch their places and their functions: people can become houses with new partners and vice versa.

The catch in all of this: there is one person too many. In the first round the person in the middle calls out 'Person' and immediately finds a house to sit in, meaning a new person will be left in the middle. This person gives another prompt, wanting to get a place as a house or person themselves.

The Princess and the Bear

A new favourite among warm-up games: pairs with their arms linked stand in the space. One pair is chosen by the game's leader and split up. One of them is the bear and the other the princess. The bear leaps towards the princess, growling like a bear, trying to catch 'her'. S/he runs away squealing. If s/he gets tired of running, s/he can link arms with one of the other pairs. Then there is a change of roles: the person on the outside (with only one arm linked) becomes the bear, and the former bear becomes the princess. If the group is very large, you can have more than one princess and bear.

Careful: socks can cause dangerous slipping! If the participants' physical abilities are too diverse, or the room is too small, then play in slow motion!

Lots of people say this is their favourite game and it is well suited for getting the group moving.

Figure 13 Workshop group in Ljubljana 2011

Figure 14 Workshop group in Ljubljana 2011

75

Irish Couples – exercise for pairs

A warm-up game in three steps:

Step 1

Two partners stand opposite each other, both holding their left hand behind their back, palms facing outward. With their right hands, each must now attempt to touch their partner's left palm, which s/he tries to prevent.

Step 2

Twist. Both partners stand opposite each other and dance the twist whilst crossing their hands on their knees. They continuously switch the hands on their knees, and at the same time they try to 'catch' their partner's knee, i.e. to tap or touch it.

Step 3

Both partners dance, hopping from one leg to the other. While they do this, they attempt to touch their partner's toe with their own toe, while trying to prevent their own toe from being touched. Careful! Be gentle with one another.

West Side Story[25] – exercise involving two groups

Two groups of the same size stand facing each other. One person declares him/herself as the leader and creates a movement and a sound intended to intimidate the opposite group, compelling them to retreat. The leader's whole group backs him/her up, imitating his/her movement and sound.

....
25 *West Side Story* is a musical by Leonard Bernstein drawing on Shakespeare's *Romeo and Juliet*. The rival gangs in this adaptation are the 'Jets' and the 'Sharks'.

Together the group drives the opposing group to the wall. Then one person in the opposing group takes the lead. Repeat this as often as is necessary for every group member to have a chance to take the lead, or as long as there is strength and desire to continue.

In many civilisations it was customary to dance 'against' each other before going into battle, until mutual respect was restored between both sides. What is it that makes this possible? Is it a test of strength? Letting your presence be known? Giving it 'your best'? Honouring our humanity, our creativity, our talents? Being true to your own essence? A 'letting yourself be seen' and a 'being seen'?

This exercise can become particularly lively when accompanied by a rousing drumbeat, and everyone can show off 'what they've got'. Once everyone has had a chance to show what they can do, peace is restored.

7. The Path to *Image Theatre*

Figure 15 *TO Vienna*, Workshop with Sanjoy Ganguly 2007

Figure 16 International Workshop Jana Sanskriti 2010

While the exercises and games up until this point have been strongly focused on experience in space, self-awareness, the recognition and questioning of our own values, strengths etc., now they move slowly in the direction of strengthening our expressive capacities. However, all the games can always be used in different contexts as warm-up games etc.

The transitions and links between the games depend upon the creativity and intuition of the facilitator.

One of the principles of 'composition' of the work sequences, can be to keep an eye on the transitions from loud to silent, from slow to fast, from lively to informative. If you can enable a workshop ethos in which these transitions are seamless, you can create what Moshe Feldenkrais calls 'mature' behaviour. We are aware of our actions at any moment and are also free to change them at any time. All possibilities are open to us, and we are not confined to just one form of expression/behaviour.

Exclusion/Inclusion

These terms are often discussed in our society, yet their meaning is determined by who is using them. The following two games symbolise the two 'concepts'; they can be played with or without an emphasis on 'being excluded'.

Exclusion

Everyone walks around in the space. The leader calls out different numbers. The number called specifies the number of people who must jointly create a static image. Those left over, are out. When leading this game, it is good not to forget the number one: then everyone creates his or her own image. The total number of people in the group could also be called.

If the game is to be played without emphasis on exclusion, then the people left over simply continue walking in the space, or stand still and observe the images made. When placing emphasis on exclusion (and how commonplace it has become for us), increasing the speed of the game highlights the 'danger' of being left out.

Inclusion

Create small circles within the group, hold hands (in fours or fives), but leave two or more people (depending on the group's size) free. The task of those who are free is to choose a random person from a group, whom they would like to catch. The chosen person's circle then has the task of protecting the person from being caught, in this case, from being touched. If the person is caught, then he or she trades places with the person trying to catch, and takes over their role.

Centre of the Universe

Take a bottle and place it in the centre of the room. Then ask the participants to stand in two rows, one on either side of the room, facing each other so that everyone stands opposite another person. Next, count along each row, each person remembering their own number. Begin counting at opposite ends such that the people with the number one are NOT standing across from one another.

The space between the two rows now symbolises the earth's surface (as though it were a flat plate), balanced on a pole, symbolised by the bottle. We are now responsible for keeping this 'earth-saucer' from tipping over. First the two people with the number one enter the playing field. Once they have begun to move they are not allowed to stop. They can move slowly or quickly, jump, crawl, dance, whatever they can think of, but they must mirror each other's position on opposite sides, and keep the 'plate' in balance.

Then the game leader calls the next number into the space, one pair after the other. Those numbers already moving must work more carefully in order to maintain their connection. Once all the players have entered the field, the leader calls out each number again in the same order, asking the pairs to leave the space as carefully as when they entered it.

Supplementary Note:

This is a very good exercise for seeing and being seen, alone, as a pair, and in the whole group, to work on something together and respond to challenges nonverbally when they arise.

Mirroring

This is a very good game to continue with. The players can remain in rows opposite each other and then step closer to one another. Your partner is now the person standing across from you.

To begin with, one row is the mirror, and the others are those who stand in front of the mirror. We start with the face and head. Make any movement you can think of, in such a way that your partner is able to mirror you as closely as possible. It is as though an invisible thread connects you. If somebody were watching you, they should hardly be able to tell which person is in front of the mirror and which person is the mirror. Next you can begin incorporating the shoulders, then the arms, your torso, and then the whole upper body! The more body parts you incorporate, the more exact you must become. Then add the hips, the pelvis and now the legs as well. Be aware of your partner's movements with your entire body.

Then allow the movements to become smaller and even more defined. And smaller and smaller, until you both once again reach a neutral position, in which your weight is evenly distributed on both of your legs and you let your arms hang.

Then switch roles!

Supplementary Note:

This exercise enables a sense of delight in concentration and trust in your own ability of expression and spontaneity. Similarly, you become fully aware of 'all your moving parts', if time allows, by moving everything (facial muscles, neck, shoulders, arms, legs etc.), one part after the other, whilst fully conscious and making sure your partner is able to follow.

The Image of the Hour

All the participants find a place in the room in which to begin the exercise. Initially each person plays on their own. It's a mime game, with no talking and without dialogue between the players. Each person focuses on his/her own experiences.

The game leader calls out the time of day and the players show what it is that they typically do at that hour. We begin at one o'clock at night. Two o'clock, three o'clock, four o'clock etc. until we arrive back at one o'clock once more. During the hours which have more activity, more time is given for nonverbal performance.

To make the group's work more interesting, we can also intersperse other, special moments into the exercise: it is Christmas time, your birthday, voting day, you read shocking news in the paper, you're doing your favourite thing.

Variation

You are allowed to have a quick look at what the others are doing. If they are doing something you prefer, then you may do it with them for a moment, before returning to your original favourite activity.

Then things continue with the normal daily schedule.

This is a good exercise for observation of our own routines and daily sequences, also offering (especially with young participants) the facilitator an opportunity to recognise what is present in their lives at the moment. For example working with 13 year-olds in a middle school, only one child did physical exercise and none ate with cutlery (right next to the school was a well known fast-food restaurant). After the workshop it was clear to the teacher that the subjects to be addressed next were health and nutrition.

Follow-up exercise

Repetitive movements: find three movements in your daily routine that you repeat frequently and learn them like choreography. Find two other people and each one teaches their choreography to the others. Then try to weave them into a new collective composition. You can also add a song or invent an accompanying sound-scape.

Supplementary Note:

This is a way of reconnecting consciously with movement patterns which have 'degenerated' into mere routines.

Playing with Balloon Puppets – exercise for pairs

Balloon puppets make a great opening exercise for the statue game or living-sculptures, as a participant recently called it.

One person is the puppet and lies down, the other one is the puppeteer. Both partners must agree on two signals, consisting of a movement and a sound. The first signal is to pump air into the puppet and inflate it, or more specifically, the body part being touched. The other signal is to let air out and the puppet / body part deflates. Off we go!

Each person in the pair plays the part of the puppet, being shaped by the air pump for roughly ten minutes before switching roles. In the last few minutes of each turn, the players can also swop their puppet for someone else's and continue playing with it.

The game is determined by the participants; principally by the capacities and the physical preferences of the one playing the puppet, and by the intentions of his/her partner.

The rules of communication, which naturally extend far beyond the two signals agreed upon, are individual and arise nonverbally from playing together.

8. Introduction to the Methods of *Image Theatre*

Figure 17 International Workshop Jana Sanskriti 2010

Figure 18 International Workshop Jana Sanskriti 2010

Figure 19 International Workshop Jana Sanskriti 2010

Image Theatre is a fundamental technique in the *Theatre of the Oppressed.*

We often assume that we are quite well versed in our language, and can normally use it to express what we think, but not always what we mean and not always so that everyone understands, since everyone has their own ideas on the words' meaning. Furthermore, language manipulates us, and we manipulate with language, for example when we use hurried polite niceties, or take on the various roles we have developed over the course of our lives. Sometimes these roles become so habitual that we confuse them with ourselves.

Bodily images however, are avowedly multidimensional and polysemic. When we create them, and then use words to comment on and interpret them, we allow the vast experience and imagination of the entire group to speak and thus become audible. An immense wealth and great diversity manifest themselves in that moment. These are also processes to generate topics within the group.

Once the diversity of the images, the range of perspectives, opinions, attitudes and experiences become visible in the groups, you can begin considering congruencies. Negotiating these is an exciting process.

Furthermore, the pathway between the eyes and brain is the shortest; when we receive information visually, we can act upon it quickly and relate to it with our knowledge and experience. In a multilingual context, working with physical images also proves itself to be an uncomplicated and direct form of communication.

Images/Building Statues

We can use people to build living statues: for this we need a volunteer. We start with a demonstration: one person acts as the artist, the other as the 'material'/ 'clay'.

Now we can shape our living statue by carefully using gentle touch to create the figure we need. Or we can 'pull' on invisible strings, as with a marionette, to move the arms and other joints or limbs in the direction we would like them to go. Or we can also use our breath, moving fingers for example, with a puff of air. We can change their facial expression by demonstrating one for them to adopt.

Finally we can also hypnotise their eyes by pointing at them with two fingers, 'dragging' them to the place we would like them to look, and fixing them there with a snap of our fingers.

Then we can whisper a sentence or phrase in their ear. And when someone looks at them, they say the phrase.

Thus one half of the group of participants become artists and the other, statues. Once everyone has finished, the artists gather and walk through the 'gallery' to admire what everybody has created. Applause! Then the roles are switched.

This method can also be used when working with many people focused on addressing certain subjects. Then the task would be, for example: create an image, using three or four people, of your views on a certain issue at your workplace, at your university, or of a project. Follow-up reflections on this are usually very fruitful. You can either create one image collectively agreed upon, or as many different images as there are people in the group.

Careful: being a statue is strenuous! Take care that it does not become too uncomfortable, and perhaps also try to remember the position/stance you are in, take a break and shake it out, and then come back to it.

The Statue Dialogue or Move by Move

To show how this game works, two people demonstrate by shaking hands and freezing in that image. Then the group is asked what they see. 'Who could these two people be?', 'In what situation?', 'What sort of relationship do they have?', 'Are they friends?', 'Is this a formal encounter?'

Then one of the two people steps out of the image and the other person stays, their now empty hand still outstretched. 'What now?', 'Who is this?', 'What does the person want?', 'Where are they?'

This first round of comments and associations by the group is intended to make us conscious that there is no obvious 'truth' in an image.

Next, everyone in the group finds a partner with whom they play the following game. The beginning is the same for everyone: two people reach for each other's hands (as though shaking hands but frozen). Then one of the two people steps out of the image, looks at how the other person is standing, and spontaneously creates a new stance in response to the image. Thus the person re-enters in such a way that the meaning of the first image is deconstructed, giving it an entirely new meaning.

Then the second person steps out of the new image, observes what is left, and then re-enters with a new idea in response.

The game is spontaneous, without speaking, and the images need not be related to produce a story.

Afterwards, once the game has been played for some time, the two partners may discuss their experiences of the game together; whether a certain dynamic or story evolved, and if so, what kind.

Variation

This game can also be played in a circle. The two people who begin with the first image of shaking hands stand in the middle. Each participant in the circle then has the chance to take the place of one of the two in the centre by touching their shoulder. This can conclude with every player entering and complementing the image, without any more substitutions. The result is one big collective image.

In this way, larger contexts can also become visible.

The Communal Image: from the real to the ideal image

The group is invited to create an image of their town, their country, their school etc.; each person who has an idea can enter the space and make a statue, which others then augment with their own. The leader asks: 'What else is there?', 'Is something still missing?'

When the image is finished, the players left over comment on it. 'What do you see?', 'What sort of atmosphere?', 'Which people?', 'What's missing?', and particularly – 'Who is missing?'

Often the absences are more significant than what is shown. In Austria, old people and children are often missing. This reveals a good deal about our society.

The Image Machine

If you like, you can also incorporate movement and sound: without leaving their places, the individual parts of the 'image of reality' can become active by making repetitive movements and sounds expressing the society's behaviour and feelings; for example, in winter, summer, in love, depressed, angry, before elections, on a normal day etc.

Tip: The instruction for this can be: 'Stay in your place, find a repeatable movement or gesture which expresses the feelings or wishes of the person you are portraying'. You can also use a word, sentence or simply make a noise. By saying 'Stop', the leader can 'calm' the machine back into a still image. The observers (those workshop participants who are not in the image) can walk around to see and hear everything closely.

Now those people on the outside can be invited to move and alter the group image, such that it corresponds to their idea of an ideal image. Is it possible to reach a consensus? Those changing the image should agree on one image in the end.

In the reflection afterwards, the insights from this process are discussed.

The *Theatre of the Oppressed* devises its scenes primarily through image creation and subsequent dynamisation. I remember a workshop with Augusto Boal in Rotterdam, in which scenes for a *Forum Theatre* piece about homophobia were being developed. In order to explore the method, two groups formed, one choosing to devise a play from their own imagination, the other using the methods of *Image Theatre* and dynamisation at the same time.

Both groups finished their work at the same time and both plays were very good and appropriate for the topic at first glance. The difference became apparent later while working with the interventions from the audience. The play that had developed organically from images[26], was structurally more coherent. Was it a coincidence? Or does our brain often interfere when we attempt to show how things present themselves to us? Try it!

In short workshops, working with images has proved useful for participants, as the images provide a receptive surface on which to project their issues.

Process Example 1

Begin with a simple image of two people standing behind one another. Then the participants are asked: 'What do you see?' The answers can be varied: standing in line waiting for an ATM, at the counter of the school cafeteria, a scene in a workplace, waiting for a bus, in line at a ticket office etc.

Then you alter the image such that the person standing behind stretches out his/her arm and points at the person in front. 'What do you see now?' Being thrown out of class, by your parents, a denunciation of someone, someone wants to hold someone back, scolding etc. 'Where could this scene take place?', 'Do you recognise this scene from your own life?'

Create an image of a conflict which you would like to work on. 'Can the others recognise the situation?', 'What could be done?', 'What would the ideal version of this situation be?', 'What is the image you'd most like to see?', 'What is necessary to change this image?' Show it in images! Then the subjects depicted can be reflected on within the group.

....
26   This process will be described in the next chapter

Process Example 2

We need three volunteers. These are now the only ones in the group who don't have to do anything. We place them such that all three stand very close to one another, but each looks in a different direction, one directly at us, others in profile. The participants sit in a half circle around the image.

'How many eyes do you see?', 'How many noses?', 'How many ears?', 'Arms?'

'Who is right?', 'How can you convince others of your 'image of reality'?', 'What is the advantage of sometimes abandoning your own standpoint?'

The exercise is short and simple and in the best cases it causes us to laugh at ourselves, when we insist too strongly on our own standpoints, and no one wants to change their own perspective, i.e. getting off your bum and walking around to see the whole situation.

If you have to cut short the *Relationship Shop* workshop at this point, because your group's time is limited (1-2 day workshop etc.), working on **Images of the Future** is an exercise which has proved itself over time, with all kinds of groups.

Images of the Future – in small groups

Using the other people in his/her group, each participant can create an image depicting what they would like their life to be like in one year's time. If it seems appropriate, you may also first depict the Real Image, and then the Ideal Image one year later.

The images are photographed and then sent to the participants. Often people place these pictures in their room, next to their beds, in a diary, to help keep their goals in mind and strive towards them. On the way, something new might develop and often small dreams give rise to bigger ones.

Excursus: Working with stories in the way Hector Aristizábal does

The Medicine Man and wise Elder of the Okanagan, said to his community:

> We have made a mistake in saying our stories are coming from the past. We are the stories. What the story does is speak in the present and bring the past forward, so we can have a future.[27]

In his work, Hector Aristizábal, who worked as a therapist for many years, combines methods from Psychodrama, ritual work and the *Theatre of the Oppressed*. In his efforts to make collective processes visible, he collects stories from all over the world, addressing subjects like initiation, guilt, healing, generational conflict, and many more; things which are present in all communities, which are distinctly human and need to be discussed if they have to be worked through.

He has contributed two of these stories: they can be found in Appendix 1 and 2 of this book.

....
27   From Awiakta, Marilou: *Selu, Seeking the Corn-Mother's Wisdom*, Fulcrum Publishing, Golden, Colorado 1993.

When he tells them, he usually uses a drum. He tells them very quickly, but loud and clear. At exciting moments he stops and asks: 'What have you understood?', 'What is it about?', 'What do you think will happen next?'

Then he continues until he has finished the story. After a short pause, allowing the story to settle, he asks his listeners to work together in small groups, creating images expressing which particular moments in the story touched them most. Then the images are presented and interpreted; i.e. the people observing them are asked whether or not they recognise the moments from the story.

In the following step, he invites the participants to transform these images into scenes from their own lives. Which elements in the image must be switched or adapted? The essence of the moment from the story and the essence of the scene from life are similar.

Afterwards, *Forum Theatre* or *Rainbow of Desire* methods may be used to continue work on the subject. I particularly like this kind of work when working with young people, since it visibly shows how people in differing phases of life, are confronted with similar challenges[28].

In his workshops, the connection across the generations, as well as the collective consciousness, is established by singing songs for the ancestors and those who have died. Incorporating the invisible elements of life invigorates and strengthens. If you do not know and can't find any songs, or don't feel comfortable with this kind of work because it is unfamiliar, then there is another way to simply bring this consciousness about: the three breaths.

....
28 For information on the concept of Transculturality, see section D.

The Three Breaths

All participants hold hands and stand in a circle. Together they take the first deep breath for those who have been here before us. Then one for the community, for our community at this time. And then a third breath for ourselves.

In this way we root ourselves in the present.

When we breathe, we can do so with our whole bodies and bend our knees, or 'gather in' the air with our arms.

9. Conclusion Part A

Closing Reflections

We create images based on our preconceptions, not only of ourselves, but of the world around us as well. Change our standpoint, and the perspective changes. If you share your ideas and perceptions with others, new possibilities always emerge.

Sometimes the truths of our bodies and those of our thinking differ. The games and exercises of the *Theatre of the Oppressed* enable us to approach ourselves, our behaviour and thinking patterns, to deliberate on them, change them, consciously hold on to them and perhaps see many things far less dogmatically. Seeing the work of others, witnessing without judgement, brings us closer to the roots of everything human.

In a concluding reflection we share with the others our insights, things that moved us, things that we question, everything that we would like to share. You can use a 'Talking Stick'[29], or an object valuable to someone, to pass from speaker to speaker. Another way to finish is by doing a dance together.

The Domino Dance

The participants stand in rows of four or five on all sides of the room. Each person is counted, and must remember their number and with whom they are in a group.

When the music starts, all the number Ones begin to move in a creative way, and as unusually as possible, through the space. After roughly 30 seconds they freeze as statues[26]. This is the cue for the number Twos in each group to start dancing.

They too freeze in a pose after a short time, but in such a way that they touch the number One in their group. Then number Three begins dancing, after s/he has frozen, number Four begins, until the entire group is reunited and has formed a collective image. Once this is done, number One can again start dancing and then freeze in a new position and space.

The groups 'travel' together through the room and continually create new images in different places.

Tip: The music for this exercise should be lively, fairly long and not too wordy.

....
29 An exercise in which a stick or object is passed from hand to hand and the person who holds it is the only one who is invited to speak.
26 Each person does this according to how they feel and in their own time.

10. Summary: Themes Part A

Touch, respect, listening, observation of group dynamics, bringing ways of ac-
quiring knowledge 'into the space' (with all our senses), awakening the 'spirit
of play', making dialogue experiential, becoming aware of our own limitations
and those of others, being in the here and now, experiencing the moment,
practising reflection.

Formulating wishes, sharing them with others, being creative together, 'gift-
ing' ourselves to others, discovering our own boundaries, exploring and enjoy-
ing shifting them.

Getting to know games and exercises from the 'arsenal' of the *Theatre of the
Oppressed,* becoming familiar with the concepts of body-memory, reawaken-
ing the various senses.

PS:

Having lunch and breaks together is an important part of theatre work!

B. Forum Theatre

Themes Part B

Text by Julian Boal: What is Oppression? How does a *Forum Theatre* play get created? Developing themes; rehearsal strategies; how does interaction with the audience work? What is a Joker? How can *Forum Theatre* be employed as a means of social transformation? Interview with Sanjoy Ganguly, founder member and leader of the Indian Theatre of the Oppressed network 'Jana Sanskriti'

1. What is Oppression?

Figure 20 International Workshop Jana Sanskriti 2010

Figure 21 International Workshop Jana Sanskriti 2010

Figure 22 International Workshop Jana Sanskriti 2010

Figure 23 International Workshop Jana Sanskriti 2010

The minimum definition of oppression, according to Augusto Boal, is that oppression exists wherever monologue replaces dialogue.

Julian Boal defines the issues addressed by the *Theatre of the Oppressed* as unjust power dynamics among different societal groups.

The text provided by Julian Boal for this book is the basis of the speech he gives at festivals, conferences and in workshops around the world.

Julian Boal – Notes on Oppression[30]

I do not want to give a final, unchangeable definition of oppression. Instead, I would like to offer grounds for a debate that I hope will be as open and contradictory as possible. Oppression is a difficult term to define, as it can unite positions and identities that, *a priori*, have few things in common: workers and homosexuals; women and colonised people; people with special needs and groups of those people considered to be 'not white'. The list is long and there is not always an evident common denominator.

A possible first definition would be to say that oppression is that which every person said to be oppressed feels. This definition may be problematic. For example, at a workshop in Switzerland that I gave with my father, a woman proposed the following theme for a *Forum Theatre* scene: she felt oppressed by the beggars who asked her for money. It may be that she felt uncomfortable or even attacked by the situation, but I believe we can agree that this is not oppression.

During a long-term workshop that *he* gave for women from villages in India, Sanjoy Ganguly[31] relates asking, 'Do any of you suffer from domestic violence, or know someone who suffers from it?' To which one woman responded, 'I don't suffer from domestic violence – my husband only beats me when it's necessary.' Is it possible that a woman beaten by her husband is only oppressed if she considers herself to be?

Another possible – and tempting – definition of oppression would be that of a set of actions between individuals. Violence, for example, would be an oppressive action in and of itself. Any victim of violence would be oppressed, and anyone who practised violence would be an oppressor.

....
30 Julian was a member of GTO-Paris. He was Augusto Boal's assistant for many years, and works throughout the world.
31 Artistic Director of the Jana Sanskriti group in Kolkata, India.

But I believe that Chen Alon, of the movement Combatants for Peace[32], as well as Edward Muallem and Iman Aoun, from Ashtar Theatre[33], would agree with me when I say that a Palestinian boy is not oppressing an Israeli soldier when he throws a stone at him. And I ask Europeans who live in countries that had an armed resistance against Nazi occupation whether they would have preferred their forebears not to have taken up arms to struggle against barbarism. Was my father an oppressor when he joined the guerrillas fighting the Brazilian dictatorship? The essentialisation of a given act – whether or not it involves violence – as belonging intrinsically to oppressors or to oppressed people tends to obscure the reasons that motivate that act.

The definition of oppression I think is most fitting is this: oppression is a concrete relation between individuals who belong to different social groups. It is a relation that benefits one group to the detriment of the other. In this attempt at finding a definition, oppression is beyond individual relationships. It is not reduced to what the English call a *'one to one relationship';* it always contains something beyond that.

Imagine a UFO that came to Earth to try to understand how cities function, and to achieve this, covered the planet – including traffic lights – with cameras. After watching the film several times, the aliens would understand that cars stop when the light turns red and start when it turns green; that pedestrians cross the street when cars stop; that cars drive on the right and pass on the left. Their film would show the rules, but it wouldn't reveal the essential question: who put the traffic light on the street? Who determines the traffic laws, and who enforces them? Who gives drivers their licenses? The state. The state, which is absolutely necessary to understanding this reality, remains invisible in the scene. The same thing happens in situations of oppression: the

....

32 A group that practises *Theatre oft the Oppressed* in Israel and Palestine, with both Palestinian and Israeli members.
33 A Palestinian group that practises *Theatre of the Oppressed* and works in Palestine and countries throughout the Middle East

relations between individuals can only be understood within the (oftentimes invisible) systems that determine them.

It is impossible to understand the relationship between a worker and a boss without understanding capitalism, just as it is impossible to understand the relationship between a white person and black person without taking racism into account, or to understand the relationship between a man and a woman without considering patriarchy.

On the other hand, there are social groups to which we do not choose to belong, and from which it is difficult – if not impossible – to release ourselves. I am a man and I live in France, which like every society in the world is patriarchal. In France, women in general make 25% less on average than men. In the same profession, with the same job description and the same experience, women make 10% less. In a relationship with a woman, I would probably make more than she did. But I am a gentleman. I would invite her to a restaurant; I would pay more of our holidays and bills, etc. I am very much a gentleman. But here we are talking about the use of power that society gives me as a man; we are not talking about equality within my relationship. And how far away is my gentlemanliness from being condescending and paternalistic?

No matter how hard I try, patriarchy will penetrate my relationship. Being an oppressor or being oppressed is not a question of individual choices, nor is it a moral question. It is also not a question of essences: no one is oppressed or an oppressor in the essence of their nature. Rather, there are social groups that relate one to another. It's an historical question. The question that ought to be asked about slavery is not whether the master is good or not, but rather, why does slavery exist? We should perhaps follow Brecht's observation: 'we worry more about the abuse of power than about power in and of itself.'

As we are all part of different social groups, we can all be oppressed and oppressors. My father always gave the example of a Chilean worker, an active member of his union who, when he went home, was a violent husband. In his relationship with his boss, this worker was, without a doubt, oppressed. But in relation to his wife, there can be even less doubt that he was an oppressor.

Speaking of oppression is not a Manichean construction of the world. The system of oppression is not a representation of the world as a confrontation between good and bad. At least in the French edition of *Games for Actors and Non-Actors,* my father dedicates the book to the oppressed classes and to the oppressed within these classes. But recognising class oppression – in other words, capitalist oppression – was never a way for my father to deny or diminish other forms of oppression.

Oppression was a term used often during the 1970s. Today, we see a profusion of other expressions, like *victim* and *excluded person.* What do they mean? A victim, as a rule, is presented as someone without the resources to confront the fate that knocks at her door, as an object for which we should have pity, someone toward whom we should feel guilt or remorse. A victim is never someone with whom we should establish solidarity or position ourselves as brothers or sisters in a common struggle.

The *tsunami* created victims, not oppressed people. An earthquake, a flood, the eruption of a volcano creates victims. But is it possible that an unemployed person is the victim of the economic crisis in the same way that someone might be the victim of lightning that strikes her on the head? The word *victim,* when used unintentionally, privileges the irrational aspect of social life and frees oppressive groups from their responsibilities.

The same applies to the word *excluded.* According to its logic, there would be no oppressors and no oppressed people, only included and excluded people.

The word *excluded* hides the causal relationship that exists between the privileges of one group and the oppression of another. No-one would be guilty of exclusion, and no-one would benefit from it. Maybe the only guilty party would be the excluded person herself. Thus, in France, we see efforts that are constantly more complex, humiliating, and authoritarian to help *excluded* people include themselves. For example, the National Employment Agency (ANPE) offers unemployed women courses in *refashioning their looks*, in which they learn to dress and make themselves up for their next job interviews. For the ANPE, then, there is no problem of unemployment in France; instead, there are too many ugly women. Society doesn't need to question itself; rather, excluded people should make more of an effort.

Another characteristic of these two terms is that they insist on the peripheral, intermittent character of injustice. The word *oppression*, on the other hand, insists on the central place of injustice in our societies' foundations.

We must recognize that there is no revolutionary romanticism in the use of the word *oppressed*. To be oppressed is a social position and not a political strategy. Within the same oppressed group, various strategies coexist. Malcolm X said that, among black American slaves, there were two groups, which he called *Field Niggers* and *House Niggers*. The *Field Nigger*, who suffered in the fields, was always ready to rebel, to try to rebel. The *House Nigger*, because he received the boss's leftovers and slept in the plantation house, could actually enjoy his position as a slave. When questioned by the *Field Nigger* as to whether he wanted to run away, the *House Nigger* responded: 'Why? We're doing so well here!' Both were oppressed by slavery, but they had different strategies. If these differences can be explained by the social diversity that exists within a group of slaves, there are also differences that are of a purely political nature. Being oppressed is not, unfortunately, any guarantee of having an appropriate strategy to fight against oppression.

Is there anything more to say about strategy? And how to defeat oppression? I would really like to know the answer. The only thing I know is that this struggle must be collective. Alone, we can elude oppression, circumvent oppression, negotiate with oppression, but never defeat it. On his own, a black man can become President of the United States without racism ending; a woman can become Prime Minister of England without patriarchy ending; a worker can become President of Brazil without exploitation ending. Defeating oppression is not the task for a hero or a messiah; it is a task for collectives, groups, organisations, masses. And in this task, theatre can help a lot, but it cannot do everything. The actor must become an activist, leave the stage and go onto the street. As my father said, *Forum Theatre* is a rehearsal for revolution or transformation, which means that it is not transformation or revolution in and of itself.

There is much more to be said about the articulation between different systems of oppression, about how racism helps capitalism, for example, or how homophobia and patriarchy combine and mutually reinforce each other. We could also approach the necessary task of defining the categories of oppressor and oppressed more precisely. For example, because I benefit from patriarchy, is it possible that I am the same kind of oppressor as a capitalist or a dictator?

When someone asked my father about a certain technical point, a certain aspect of methodology, what to do in a certain situation, or if it was possible to do one thing or another, he responded many times that methods were made for people, and that people were not made for methods. But what people were the methods made for? For oppressed people, always. How, then, to define who is the oppressed, who is the oppressor, and establish strategies to obtain the opposite of oppression, which is emancipation? These questions cannot be avoided, because they are what permit us to distinguish *Theatre of the Oppressed* from a cultural diversion for excluded people, or occupational therapy for victims.

To respond to these questions, my father's legacy is fundamental, but not sufficient. It was never sufficient. My father continually supported what he called creative heresies, which he always distinguished from unpardonable betrayals. From here, we have the difficult task of reconciling faithfulness with creativity.

– End of Julian Boal's text. –

Figure 24 Julian Boal 2010

Thus Julian Boal. In the TO context he has spent a great deal of time thinking about this concept and in this text he deals with the key aspects of the problem. To speak of oppressed and oppressor does not mean drifting into sterile polarisation, to see things in black and white, or to get stuck in an outmoded 19th-century jargon-ridden Marxist structure. It is rather a working model for confronting a complex reality.

It may be that outside Europe, in the global South, in the sweat shops of the world, oppression shows itself more clearly and we in Europe are better at covering it up. But it spreads its countless tentacles into all realms of life and all places. The crassest form of selective vision in European society must be the way we treat asylum seekers and the human trafficking which accompanies it. Racism, sexism and patriarchy are themes which are brought up throughout the world when discussing oppression.

Nevertheless the title *Theatre of the Oppressed* is an obstacle for many people and I have often been present when Augusto or Julian have been asked by project organisers, workshop participants or journalists whether it would be advisable to change the name.

The reason behind this was always the concern whether this method could be 'successful' and 'popular' and, above all, whether it would be possible to attract money for projects under this name. Augusto's answer was always the same. He would ask: 'But do you find oppression here? If so, the name of our theatre and its employment are justified.'

Above and beyond that, the name *Theatre of the Oppressed* refers back to Paulo Freire's 'Pedagogy of the Oppressed'. It is a tribute to the great Brazilian popular educator, who, along with Augusto Boal, was awarded an honorary doctorate from the University of Nebraska in 1996. Augusto Boal said repeatedly in many places: 'For me to exist, Paulo Freire has to exist'. That also means that *Theatre of the Oppressed* offers a chance to engage with the historical moment of its genesis, an invitation to read Freire and to carry his insights forward into the 21st-century and build upon them. Be warned: there are side-effects! Activist theatre practice widens horizons. And it's fun...!

Theatre of Human Rights

In his attempt to forge a common identity among the many *Theatre of the Oppressed* activists across the world, Augusto Boal identified the International Declaration of Human Rights as the modern basis of our theatre movement.

This declaration, signed by all members of the UN in 1948, legitimises the aspiration to 'humanise humanity'.

Theatre of the Oppressed, this great international movement, active in five continents, in dozens of countries, in centres, groups and individuals, which reaches hundreds of thousands of people, is working towards a society which would function in accord with this Declaration of Human Rights. That is our identity and our legitimacy.

The only problem is that no-one reads it, no-one follows it and only a few people even know it exists. We ought to read it, because it contains, set out in 30 articles, basic rights whose aim is to ensure human happiness. In a video, Augusto Boal says:

> We should write it down somewhere so that everyone is clear: *Theatre of the Oppressed* is against torture and in favour of paid holidays. Slavery is prohibited. As ever, governments fail to respect these principles. The concept of legitimacy is associated with the concept of legality. But in fact it's not quite the same thing. Legality is a composite derived from laws, habits, traditions and culture, which constructs everyone's moral horizon, but it is not restricted to this. For the ethical notions which underpin morality are always in process of changing, both in the domain of work and in relationships. Ethical behaviour is always a little removed from us, it is a goal. Morality (Latin: *mores*) relates to everything which already exists and is accepted unquestioningly by the majority. Ethics (Greek: *ethos*) is what one desires for oneself and for the human race.

What do we desire? That the UN Declaration of Human Rights should be respected, followed and carried out. It was originally intended to be a [universal] law, but it still only represents a utopian dream, which needs to be lived.[34]

And as far as human rights are concerned it is a similar picture to the issue of democracy: what we are living are laborious approaches to it. As I have discovered over years in *Forum Theatre* and human rights workshops with Walter Suntinger[35] and as Julian Boal describes in his essay, events and actions cannot be reduced to a common essence without evaluating the underlying causes and the specific contexts which produce them.

And working for human rights reminds us of our responsibility to take an active role in bringing them to general attention.

Becoming the author of our own story – Scripting the Play instead of Playing the Script

So much could be written on this theme![36]

Working in the tradition of liberation art and pedagogy cannot be divorced from the political events and the resultant currents of the second half of the last century. Our theatre has grown organically and this span of time is the soil from which it has sprung. Nodal points are the *Cuban Revolution*, *Liberation Theology*, the *Pedagogy of the Oppressed* and what is known as *committed art and science*.

---

34 Augusto Boal, *On Human Rights*, CTO Archive, Rio de Janeiro.
35 Austrian human rights lawyer who works internationally.
36 See particularly Sanjoy Ganguly 2010, Chapter 7

An individual who was very prominent in this respect in Latin America was Orlando Fals Borda, the first Columbian sociologist. He was also much more than that, but that is outside the scope of this book, so I will merely indicate that the Bibliography contains information about work by and about him.[37]

More or less at the same time as the Latin American artists, among them Augusto Boal, came out strongly in favour of a People's Theatre free from European influence and put this into practice, Fals Borda committed himself to a new and more independent brand of historical writing and research.

> We must bind (theoretical) study and (practical) action together, in order to contest the condition of dependency and exploitation which has characterised and determined us with all its degrading consequences and oppressive mechanisms. This can be clearly seen in our culture of imitation and poverty and in the lack of social and economic participation which typifies our people.[38]

Here he is alluding to the fact that it is always a select few who determine WHAT culture is, WHO can participate and, when one looks at previous research studies, or indeed in many places present ones as well, who is profiting from the activity of whom. As the members of the agricultural worker's movement Jana Sanskriti frequently say with pride: 'we have made several PhD theses possible'.

The most interesting work of Fals Borda in this respect was the *Historia doble de la Costa* ('The Double History of the Coast'), in which he developed an investigative methodology for social science[39] which as a conscious political strategy included input from the actors (the 'subjects of investigation') rather

....

37   He originated Participatory Action Research
38   Fals Borda, Orlando, *Über das Problem, wie man die Realität erforscht, um sie zu verändern* ('On the problem of doing research into reality in order to change it'), in Moser H. & Ornauer H., Eds., *Internationale Aspekte der Aktionsforschung.* Köbel, München 1978, pp. 78-112.
39   Investigación Acción Participativa/Participatory Action Research (PAR)

than degrading them to the status of objects. In this way the consciousness of the investigator was naturally altered. Augusto Boal went through a similar process whereby his theatre developed from a theatre of answers (propaganda theatre) to a theatre of questions.

The basic traits of this kind of research are very similar to what in theatre we call *collective creation* or *co-creation*.

The results of both these 'research foci', sociology and theatre, bring together space and time, present and past, the voices of the researchers and of those being investigated; and a picture emerges of a living culture, which in face of industrialisation (recently) and globalisation (now) cannot be reduced to what it never was and hopefully never will be, a banal and oversimplified single entity.

Not only since 1992 (500 years after the 'discovery' of America) have the questions 'whose history are we learning?', 'who writes it?', 'through whose eyes do we see it?' been asked across the world.

They are also what we deal with in theatre. Firstly it is important to tell our own story and secondly to view and to understand it as a part and in the context of a larger, collective history.

2. Summoning up content

The following games and exercises are the first stages of a process which we call generating material or summoning up content. In a variety of ways they touch on forms of collective knowledge, social structures, rituals and taboos, and provide a pool of thematic material which can later be incorporated at appropriate points into the construction of *Forum Theatre* plays. Furthermore they sensitise the performers to aspects of our life which have hitherto remained latent.

Good Cop/Bad Cop – exercise for three people

The theme of this exercise is interaction with language. Its aim is to de-couple HOW something is said from WHAT is said.

Two players provide suggestions which the third – keeping his/her eyes closed – has to turn into mime. The first two have to choose whether to be nice or nasty. Nice suggestions (e.g. 'eat up your favourite food!'; 'dream of something beautiful!'; 'lie down in the sun!') have to be delivered in an unpleasant, aggressive tone, while the nasty ones (e.g. 'take a cold shower!') are said in a very friendly and benevolent way.

Swop roles three times so that each player plays each role.

Follow this with a discussion about the manipulative use of language, the functioning of small talk and polite remarks in social situations, as well as the business of 'meaning well'.

The two revelations of Saint Theresa – exercise for pairs

The theme of this exercise is social taboos. The partners decide first which roles they will play in an improvisation using speech and movement. It must be about an important relationship between two people, for instance parents and children, best friends, worker and boss, siblings, partners in a relationship etc.

They decide on the place where they usually meet and begin the improvisation. After a while the leader gives the signal: 'first revelation!' Then the first person (they need to choose at the beginning who will be first and who second) reveals something to the second which will completely change the nature of their relationship. The secret is something which emerges spontaneously from the improvisation.

Then the improvisation continues for the next few minutes and the players have to incorporate this information.

Then the leader says: 'second revelation!' Then person number two tells number one a secret, some circumstance, some truth, which once more changes the relationship fundamentally.

The game goes on for a few more minutes. Then the group shares what the secrets were about. Often they have to do with issues like parenthood, faithfulness, money, affairs, revelations about family connections, sexual orientation: themes which are difficult to talk about in many societies.

Once in a workshop I forgot to point out that this game should be about real people. As a result one participant told her partner: 'I am the Goddess!' Whereupon the second participant revealed: 'And I'm an atheist and I'm sorry to inform you that you don't exist!'

Figure 25 *TO Vienna*, Creación Colectiva with Carlos Zatizabal 2009

Status exercise 1 – 7

Theme: social class

In this game, in which the whole group participates, the theme is social class. Participants stand or sit in a circle, whose configuration symbolises social space. The leader gives each participant, one after another, a number between 1 and 7, which the latter then have to materialise as a role or character. Number 1 is the most important, the most powerful, number 7 is the least important and least powerful (e.g. 5 is a supermarket cashier, 3 a teacher, 6 a building worker etc.).

These mimed presentations are not commented on, simply observed (the interpretations of the different numbers are sometimes very different, some people would see an artist as 1 whereas others would opt for a CEO). When everyone has shown their role, there is a whole-group improvisation. Everyone walks around the room in role, at first still just miming, without engaging in dialogue with the others.

Then they start to voice their 'inner monologue' for a while, i.e. they speak aloud the thoughts of the person they are representing. Everyone imitates the actions of the person they are representing and they also try now to establish contact. 'For whom did this work?' 'Who didn't feel it worked?' 'What kind of social contact occurred through playing out this reality?'

The game carries on for as long as it goes on being engaging and productive, and then in a circle everyone says what they experienced and what they felt about the game. If the group is very homogenous – e.g. with students, who have had little or no experience of the workplace, the game is sometimes judged a failure. But even that can be interesting.

The ABC exercise

Here the theme is personal priorities and things one avoids. Everyone walks around the room. Think of someone in the room! This person is now A for you. A is particularly important. Wherever you are in the room, you should know exactly where A is in relation to you. Without forgetting A, think of a second person in the room. This person is now B. B is also important, but not as important as A. Out of the corner of your eye you are always aware that B is there too. And now think of a third person. From now on this person is C. C is so much in the background that you don't want to see her or be seen by her. Keep moving for a while with this consciousness of A, B and C. Stop!

Now get into small groups and discuss. What does A represent in your life? What could B symbolise? And very difficult and interesting: what does C mean for you? An example could be things like good health, family, environment, sustainable life, financial insecurity, age, inclusion/exclusion, creativity etc.

To give a concrete example, if A is my family, perhaps B is my health and C the feeling I have about how far I am realising my potential, which has perhaps got a bit stuck.

Images of Oppression

Figure 26 Kyrgyzstan Workshop 2006

The group sits in a circle. Everyone is asked to take on the role of an oppressed person in a concrete situation of oppression in society. Half the group are asked to show their images (individually, but all at the same time); then the other half are invited to adopt the role of an oppressor for one of the images and to take up that position: in this way pairs are formed.

Then the pairs begin to improvise, without discussing whether or not they have 'understood' each other's image. At first the improvised interactions between oppressor and oppressed are done as mime, without words, just actions. Then with sounds. Right at the end, improvised text is added. Then the exercise ends with group discussion.

Variation 1

During the mime interaction the leader can call for a freeze and get everyone to speak their inner monologue for a short while. Then go back to mime.

Variation 2

The person representing the oppressed figure also creates the image of the relevant oppressor. If anyone in the audience 'understands' this role and the image it gives rise to, he or she can take on the role, replacing the original player.

Tell participants: Never put others into the role of the oppressed, only yourself. It is your decision to work on the theme, others can only be invited to take part and support the telling of the story.

3. One of the many ways to *Forum Theatre*

For many reasons, Augusto Boal preferred non-verbal, bodily expression as the starting-point for developing scenes for *Forum Theatre*[40].

One reason for this is that it is a very good way of opening up the path from an individual story (which enriches, informs and enlivens the play) towards the development of a story which represents collective experience and enables us to explore with the audience the issues which affect us all and through which we recognise our own reality.

Our collective and individual experiences are stored in our bodies and we can call them up from there. Speech on the other hand inhibits our imagination, because for the most part we only use it to reformulate what we already

....
40   With other techniques it is different, e.g. with Rainbow of Desire work stories are often told as well. Rainbow work has a different focus and is often more introspective.

know. We want to use theatre to help us to break free of this mechanical process.

Excursus: Making images from fairy-tales

In a variety of cases I lead up to *Forum Theatre* work by making images from fairy-tales. With cross-cultural groups particularly, but also when working with children, this produces very good results and is a rapid introduction to *Image Theatre* work.

The task is to agree on a myth or fairy-tale in the group and to depict this as a story in pictures, using at least 5-7 images.

The fairy-tale must be kept secret until it is shown to the others. When the picture stories are being shown, I ask the audience to shut their eyes whilst one image is being changed into the next[41]. Then the audience is asked to say what it has seen. The actors can only react to the comments at the end and must listen to everything first. It's not about guessing the tale, but about WHAT people have seen and what comes out of sharing this.

With homogenous groups it may be possible to discuss the meaning of fairy-tales in our life in the reflection session[42] (for example, the 'wicked wolf' who is constructed to function as a source of anxiety to girls and young women with lasting impact, a figure which is evoked with great glee in all sorts of formats[43]), whilst in heterogenous groups the different interpretations are fascinating[44].

....

41 'Eyes closed!' 'Eyes open!' At the beginning I ask groups how many images there are in their stories.
42 There were workshops where we had three different versions of *Red Riding Hood*.
43 Trade-mark pitch: 'Are you travelling alone? Aren't you scared?'
44 Once a bible story was interpreted as a neo-liberal conflict model.

The path to *Forum Theatre* in ten steps – small group work

Figure 27 *TO Vienna*, Creación Colectiva with Carlos Zatizabal 2009

Step 1 – Choosing the Subject

Four to six players form a group. Then each one thinks of an oppressive situation, a conflict, or unjust power relationship that touches or interests him/her. Then they show them using still images.

Each player is author of one image, using the people from his or her group to create it. Finally, the author places him or herself in the role of the oppressed person, the protagonist.

The group remains in the image long enough to commit it to memory, before the next person creates another image. In the end, there are as many images as there are players.

Once everyone has made an image, the group can reflect on each image together. First, the players who were positioned in the image can say how they understood the author's intention, based on the shape they were put in. Then the author of the story can tell the group what he or she wanted to express with the image.

The next group task is to choose an image, or subject, which they would like to continue working with. This may be a synergy of different images that emerged in the preceding process, or simply one of the images, or an entirely new image. But it is crucial that all of the group members agree on the relevance of the issue.

Variation

If you find yourself under time pressure, and are working with a homogenous group which has 'got up a lot of steam' (i.e. a great deal of emotional turmoil) – depending on their age – the group can simply be asked to create an image of their conflict situation and then perform it straight away.

Step 2 – The Other's Associations

The images chosen by the groups are looked at. Just as with the work in the first part of the book, using the 'real-image' the facilitator asks the group: 'What do you see?', 'What is happening here?', 'Who are the people involved?', 'What kind of atmosphere is being expressed here?'

The group showing their image just listens and bears in mind what they hear from the viewers, as material for developing their topic into a scene. They should not try to explain what they meant.

Step 3 – The Image Series/Story

The original image is now fanned out into a series of five to seven images, creating a story. They must ask themselves: 'What happened before the moment of our image?', 'Where is the scene taking place?', 'Who are the people involved?', 'Who else is there?', 'What happens next?', 'What consequences emerge from the conflict?', 'What does the protagonist want?'

Step 4 – The Slow Motion Silent Movie

Now the images from the extended sequence are put together in the form of a silent movie performed in slow motion. Slow motion gives the necessary space for the characters' emotions and reactions to become visible as they transition from one image or situation to the next.

Step 5 – Stop and Think – The inner Monologue

In the next step, all the groups (or just the group if there is only one) perform the slow motion silent movie version of their scene.

The leader interrupts the sequence several times by clapping his/her hands and shouting 'STOP! THINK! (or INNER MONOLOGUE!'[45]).

Upon hearing this direction, all the players freeze immediately and begin to speak out loud the inner monologue (or alternatively 'Stream of Consciousness'), of the person they are portraying. Their physicality in that moment informs the text they speak. The longer they speak, the more information will emerge.

---

45 The performer is trying to subjectively reproduce perceptions, thoughts, feelings and reflections of the character they are playing as they pass through her/his consciousness.

Then the pantomime-like slow motion silent movie performance continues. This procedure is repeated several times. At the end of this round of work, the group reflects on the most important insights gained for the scene.

Step 6 – The text – The most important arguments – The main motivation – The protagonist's desire

If there are enough people available, then one person per group can be asked to note down the most important information that emerges during the STOP and THINK, and later recount this to the others.

The next step is to identify and express, as concretely as possible, the main arguments of those involved and the protagonist's desire. The aim is to produce the first draft of a script.

It can be helpful to find between three and five sentences for each person, which are most important for their role.

Step 7 – Everyone plays every part once

In *Forum Theatre* work, particularly with new groups, it is important that a role does not become 'stuck' on one person. Moreover, all of us have had varying life experiences in varying situations, so it is always good and enriching to trade roles and see how someone else approaches a challenge. Each role-swop brings about new possibilities!

By the time they move on to the next step, the group should have already chosen the most important sentences for each role; the rest can be improvised.

The roles are traded as many times as there are players in the scene, and so there are the same number of run-throughs of the scene. After each run-through the group reflects on what was new, how people played the roles differently, what went particularly well, what should be kept, what was too much, and how things should continue. This selection process produces a working script, meaning a text and a corresponding scene sequence. Don't worry: the piece will continue to change as you work; the existing 'material' is a foundation that will be carved and adjusted, scrapped and amended. It represents a preliminary consensus within the group to address the question expressed in the scene.

Now we continue with the rehearsal techniques, which in turn address different levels of scene development.

Step 8 – An ABC of Rehearsal Techniques

You can find an abundance of exercises and suggestions on how to devise and flesh out scenes in Boal's book *Games for Actors and Non-Actors*. They help improve the various dimensions (developing roles, coherence of the plot, expression) of the scene. To make the work somewhat easier, Augusto Boal once showed us 15 techniques which are sufficient for a start. There is no right or wrong sequence of application, it is a toolbox from which one can pick whatever appears useful. However, each exercise enriches and expands the play, making it more informative, so we usually use at least 10 to 15. If possible, it is helpful to have an observer present. He/she notes the interesting things which emerge during improvisation, which can later be integrated into the piece.

Exploring the Characters

a) Stop and Think – The Most Important One

The first method of in-depth character is the one mentioned in step five, *Stop and Think*. Now, as the scene has developed further and the sequence of events has taken a clearer form, we repeat the exercise in order to obtain additional, in-depth information from the players' stream of consciousness.

Again it is useful to have one person observing from the sidelines, noting down important key words from the improvised monologues. The scene is played, the leader/director once again gives a signal to freeze: 'Stop'; and to begin speaking the thoughts of the character out loud: 'Think'.

After the end of the exercise, you may again have a round of reflection in which the new insights are integrated into the gradually developing piece.

b) Analytical Rehearsal of Emotions

The entire scene, using the text that has been decided upon, is now played in just one emotional mood. This means, for instance, that everyone plays as though they were in love (or jealous, mean, angry, depressed, in a good mood, apprehensive etc.) and maintains this throughout the whole scene. On the one hand, this leads to interesting contradictions, which in turn help stabilise people in their roles by challenging them. On the other hand, meaningful moments begin to emerge as the emotion 'falls into place', which in turn helps the actors sense the point at which precisely this emotion fits well (in this exercise, emotions are chosen because they are important for the piece). You can then keep it there as you continue to develop the play.

c) Analytical Rehearsal of Style

In this rehearsal technique, the entire piece/entire scene is performed in a particular style or genre. Here, divergent styles, which have nothing to do with the piece, are helpful. For example: a Mexican soap opera, classical ballet, Opera, Crime Show, pulp novel etc. The resulting strangeness once again gives the actors a chance to develop an analytical distance from the action, and thus greater freedom and depth in their performance.

d) The Hannover Variation

This rehearsal technique needs an audience. The scene is played and if someone in the audience has a question for the characters, then they raise their hand. Once enough hands are in the air, the leader stops the performance and the audience begins bombarding the various characters with their questions. In doing so, it is important for them to be familiar with the names of the characters, as their questions should be addressed directly at those individuals portrayed in the piece. The questions should be as intimate and surprising as possible, so that they truly challenge the actor in developing his or her role. The actors must react on the spot 'extempore' and answer in a manner that is coherent and appropriate to their role. The most amazing insights can be gained from this exercise.[46]

e) Animals

Before they begin, all the actors think of an animal most akin, in terms of character, to the person they are portraying in the play. They do not reveal to one another which animal they have chosen. As the performance progresses, they then become more and more like this animal, while still speaking the same text. Initially there might only be a light scratching or a meagre flapping of wings, but by the end they openly hiss, pant and chase. This exercise is normal-

....
46   During a workshop in Rotterdam with Augusto Boal, for a play about the bullying of a homosexual teacher, an entire class of students once admitted their fascination for same-sex love.

ly very lively and often impassioned, and like the previous techniques, it helps the actors in their role development.

To improve expressivity

a) The Ceremony

In this run-through, all the actors play their roles as though every one of their actions were of the utmost importance and meaning. While doing so, they take up as much space as possible, command the attention of all the performers with their gaze, and give their actions the state of solemn ritual. This technique is a study of expression, and helps the actors to identify the truly important, concrete actions, since everything secondary becomes redundant and thus falls away.

b) The Silent Movie

This technique, which we already used in step four, also needs an audience. The scene is played like a silent movie. Subsequently, the audience comments on WHAT it saw, and the actors listen. Thereby, they get critique and feedback on WHAT they wanted to show, and on what they actually expressed through their actions. In this kind of rehearsal, it is helpful to already have all the props and to have chosen the costumes, as these also carry part of the visual information.

c) The Reconstruction of the Crime

In this scene rehearsal, each actor announces what she/he will do before she/he does it. This method allows an exact reconstruction of the action sequence, so that the important elements become clear.

d) Rashomon

This technique, which gets its name from Akira Kurosawa's film, allows the exploration of the action from various perspectives, by those involved in it. Each person in the piece designs an action sequence in which she/he sculpts the others as statues, expressing how she/he sees this person from her/his perspective. Finally, the person sculpts her/himself to express the way s/he sees her/his own role in the piece.

The scene is then to be played while trying to retain the statue shape as well as possible. This means that there are as many run-throughs as there are people in the scene.

This rehearsal method makes it clear how the people in the play see each another (as a monster, as a scaredy-cat etc.), as well as exposing the varying levels of relationship present.[47]

e) Somatic Study

The scene is played under unusual physical prerequisites: women perform as though they were men and vice versa, everyone performs as though they were underwater, or in a desert storm, on icy ground, or hanging on a cliff, or while being attacked by ants etc. This technique also helps to concentrate on the essentials and to express them more clearly.

....

47 In one scene addressing bullying in a school, there was a couple that often made themselves the centre of attention. The girl placed her boyfriend and herself on a table in the classroom, like models being admired by the rest. When the actor playing her boyfriend sculpted the scene, she found herself kneeling on the floor in front of him, while only he remained on the table.

Dramatising the Scene

a) I don't believe you!

The scene is played, and every time an actor feels that the behaviour of one of her/his partners is not convincing, s/he can interrupt the action and say: 'I don't believe you!' (or: 'I don't buy that!'). The actor challenged must then do everything in her/his power to convey the desired message in a convincing manner. If s/he manages this, then the play can go on.

b) Secret

The scene is played as though everything happening were one big secret. All the actors whisper and attempt to convey all of their emotions through gesture, facial expression and physicality. This heightens the tension of the scene, and the concentration of the actors.

c) What???

If an actor cannot be heard by her/his fellow players, then one of them can throw in a 'What did you say?' or 'What was that?' Then the last thing said must be repeated loud and clear.

d) Far away

All the actors in a scene stand as far apart as possible within the space. The scene however, is played as though they were as close to each other as they were originally. But they must remain far away from each other. This exercise leads to great intensity of expression and increased vocal effort. It is particularly nice when several scenes are being rehearsed at the same time, in the same room, using this method and everyone is scattered all over the space.

e) Long Beach Telegram

Only the most important word in each sentence may be spoken. But the entire meaning of the sentence should still be conveyed. This results in the text being spoken with great emotional intensity, and gestures slowed down so that they become more interesting.

The outcomes of these rehearsal techniques are reflected upon and then flow into the piece. You may use as much – or sometimes as little – time as is available. What is important is the appreciation of the value of the aesthetic in the language of theatre, as a way of communicating meaning. If you don't explore artistic expression as fully as possible, many possibilities will remain unrealised.

What this means: Work with any and all imaginable tools: music, dance, singing, prologue, stage design, costumes, decorating the venue according to the theme, masks, puppets etc. Moreover, theatre can make the invisible visible; this may occur through realistic or surreal means (e.g. dream sequences, playing out memories, scenes from mythology, from the narratives of a society).

Step 9 – The Dramaturgy of *Forum Theatre*

The dramaturgy of a *Forum Theatre* play should be as clear as possible. This is the only way in which the spectactors will be able to find their way around it. This does not mean that a subject should be made banal, but rather, creating a framework in which it is possible to get to grips with the topic. Whether or not a production is considered banal – and this is very important – is very dependent on the work of the Joker or Kuringa, and the questions s/he poses. The production should thus be seen as just one part of a whole.

Forum Theatre is always a collective intellectual and emotional examination of an issue by the actors and the audience. The issue can be very complex, but may also have very simple traits; in both cases it is good if it matches the needs and capacities of the actors.

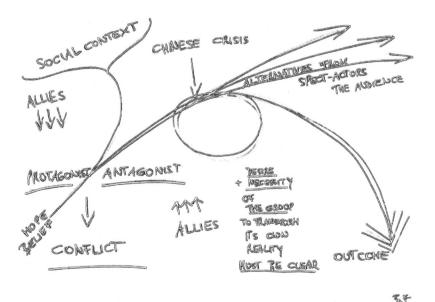

Figure 28 The Dramaturgy of the *Forum Theatre* Play

The nature of the protagonist's and antagonist's characters must be very clear. On both sides there are potential allies, which can represent windows and doors for the audience. They can be used by the spectactors to break out of the oppression, challenging the allies to change their attitude and behaviour.

The original scene is structured around a conflict in which the protagonist cannot pursue her/his ambitions, belief structure, or wishes, because the antagonist's will is stronger.

The climax of the action brings with it the *Chinese Crisis.* It is Chinese because the Chinese word for crisis uses the characters which signify both *danger* and *opportunity.* This is the moment that offers the audience a chance to influence the outcome of the action, according to their wishes.

However, prior to this, it is important that the characters involved in the action are able to clearly express their own needs and the justification for them, such that the direction in which the reality must shift is clear. *Forum Theatre* is thus an ethical theatre which articulates very clear standpoints. Augusto Boal also called it the *Theatre of Human Rights.*

Bárbara Santos says on this point:

> If there is a *necessity* for change but no personal *motivation* for change is present, that means that those affected are in a state of depression. If the *desire* for change is present but there is no real *need* for it, this leads to *charity* and *heroism.* These should both be avoided, because they sideline the autonomy and will of those affected.[48]

There are objective conflicts with a subjective component and subjective conflicts with an objective component. And there are *antagonistic conflicts*, e.g. between a worker and her supervisor, and *non-antagonistic conflicts*, e.g. be-

---

48   This is particularly important in the case of NGO theatre projects.

tween a daughter and her mother. It's important to be aware of these components and paradigms and to keep them in mind.

Forum Theatre needs to articulate the hopes and desires of the protagonists and provide them with an identity which is solidly based. Beyond that, it is the art of saying 'No'. No to situations which we don't agree with, which we want to change.

The Scenes

Whilst researching another book, I came across an anecdote about Augusto Boal and the development of *Forum Theatre*. Unfortunately I've lost the exact reference, but I remember that it had to do with a theatre group in a district of a large town in the USA, which Augusto Boal had worked with when he was shaping his first *Forum Theatre* plays. His plays at that time were always very long and thorough and the opportunity for interventions from the audience happened right at the end. The group – I think it was from the Bronx – changed the structure and developed plays which only lasted 15 minutes. They said to Augusto: 'See Augusto, we live in a neighbourhood which is speedy and dangerous and stressful. We want to really reach people. Nobody here has the time to spend a whole hour watching a play. But 15 minutes, that's OK.'

What this shows is that it's important to know your audience and to find ways to work with themes so that they can still be portrayed realistically and don't slide into superficiality, but also to pay attention to what one has to do to attract an audience, how, as it were, to develop it and how to meet it on its own territory.

For street theatre it's sometimes a case of just using still images which we want to involve the audience in changing, often in combination with *Newspaper Theatre* or *Invisible Theatre*.

134

Alternative: *'Blind' Forum or 'blank' Forum*

Blank Forum is an exercise in which an obstacle, whose origins are not revealed, has to be overcome. The images which are presented function as surfaces on which to project the oppressions which the players are suffering from. By playing them out it is possible to overcome them[49]. Blind Forums are a good preparation for *Forum Theatre* work as well as good research tools for identifying and working on problematic scenarios in communities. My favourite scenario is:

It's too late!

On the stage there are three tables, each with a chair and a person sitting at each one. The protagonist runs up to the first table. The person sitting at the first table stands up and says: 'Too late'. The protagonist returns to the start, slightly uneasy. Then s/he takes courage and goes to the second table. The person there also says: 'Too late'. Frustrated, the protagonist goes back to the starting point. This time s/he doesn't run, but walks up to the third table. As s/he gets there, the person sitting there turns away and s/he too says: 'Too late'.

What would you do in the protagonist's place?

In the subsequent interventions by other people in the group, everyone interprets the situation in their own way and tries to find a relevant solution to the problem, however they interpret it. The images of the table and chair and the seated occupant serve as a kind of empty frame which awakens a range of dormant images of oppression from within the group (often they relate to situations from school, from the workplace, from love relationships, from hospital, etc.).

....
49   A 'playing cure', not just a 'talking cure' then, to give a Viennese reference (translators' note).

We used this game in the following way with a group from Venezuela. We allowed the participants to choose an everyday situation corresponding to the basic structure and as a group they decided on a scene about a family member, who has to fetch some medicine urgently from the chemist for another sick member.

No chemist was willing to help, for various reasons: one tried to bluster and ask for more than his due; another didn't stick to the advertised opening hours; the weekend service didn't operate properly; the information in the newspaper about the emergency rota was inaccurate; the medicine, although quite common, hadn't arrived because of industrial action.

In a very short time we had come up with a Forum about the provision of healthcare facilities in the country, and started a passionate debate on why things were not working.

Step 10 – Forum – That's What It's About!

The rules of the game

The play is shown once. At the beginning the Joker greets the audience and gives a brief outline of what is going to happen. The rule of thumb is: less is more.

The Joker is not on stage for the first showing. For everything else he or she should be clearly visible to the audience and should act as the anchor.

After the first run it is advisable to give the audience a bit of time to digest what they have seen. One way of doing this is to invite people to exchange views briefly with their neighbours about the conflict they have seen and to think together about possible solutions.

When it has gone quiet in the room and you feel the time is right, the Forum phase begins.

Now the spectators – Boal calls them **spectactors** – have the chance to take over the role of the protagonist and to re-direct the action which happened onstage so that it leads to what they see as a positive outcome. So they need to decide which moment they want to begin from.

The play starts again and when someone has an idea, he or she can call out 'Stop!' Then the action is halted and that person replaces the protagonist on stage. To help, they normally get a distinctive piece of costume or a prop which signals the role.

The other actors now have to react spontaneously to the alternative course of action proposed by the spectactor, whilst sticking as closely as possible to their character.

As a *Forum Theatre* actor, one is always simultaneously in role and also part of the directorial process, which means that it is a dual task. In addition one has to respond sensitively to the person who has come on stage by gauging the right degree of resistance or of oppression to employ in opposition to what they propose, in order to bring out as much as possible of what they can offer, without overpowering them.

When a spectactor has shown his/her intervention, either the Joker or the spectactor stops the play, and s/he is given a round of applause. Following the intervention the Joker discusses with the audience what they have seen. There are as many interventions as members of the audience come up with and that can either go on as long as it takes to get through them, or until the house manager switches off the lights.

After that the Joker sums up the interventions which have come up and puts them in the context of the theme of the play, and then all the actors and spec-tactors get a round of applause[50].

4. Jokering the *Forum Theatre* play

Forum Theatre plays deal with oppressed and oppressors and that is already a lie. The world isn't divided into right and wrong, we all know that.

One day we are on one side, the next we are on the other. We all carry traces of both in us. We are even born into a world which makes us into one or the other without our knowledge for long periods of our life.

No-one knew that better than Augusto Boal, and as the political history of Bra-zil in recent times shows, those who were absolute 'underdogs' in one decade can rise to the heights of power. Who would have thought in the 1970s that Lula would one day be President[51]? Or have predicted the same for Nelson Mandela? Or have foreseen that Augusto Boal would be nominated for the Nobel Peace Prize?

Forum Theatre is, as Adrian Jackson[52] likes to say, 'a safe place to disagree'. We live today in a strange world, which claims to be interested in consensus whilst manifesting enormous injustices. Particularly in cases where the oppressed have accepted their role and say things like: 'My husband isn't really bad to me. He only beats me when I deserve it'[53] or in a European context: 'Women don't earn less than men here. Men just earn a little bit more'.[54]

....

50 Jana Sanskriti document all interventions; it is also useful to do this and draw up a list of potential subsequent ac-tions, particularly if it is intended to develop towards *Legislative Theatre*.
51 Luiz Inácio Lula da Silva
52 Artistic Director of Cardboard Citizens, who work principally with the homeless in London using TO: see www.cardboardcitizens.org.uk
53 cf. Julian Boal's essay (pp. 102-108)
54 Quotation from Sweden

When we act as Jokers for *Forum Theatre* plays, we can be sure that it is more interesting to have a variety of opinions, that we do not all hold the same view, that a plurality of different opinions can be healthy and can contain possibilities of learning from each other.

Forum Theatre is a practical way to achieve solidarity, can be used to address real-life situations and also has a symbolic value: to name 'the crime'.

The perfect scene is a conflict between two people. The background is the social context of the conflict. We begin with the microcosm and transfer the issue to the macrocosm. People are also the products of a system, a little scene therefore always represents more than appears at first sight.

For this there is no single recipe, but lots. It is important for the spectators to be able to see what the protagonist sees and can complement his or her perspective. It's not that they should have any kind of magic powers, but that the dramaturgy of the play should be so clear that the necessity and the desire for it to be turned into action can be clearly presented. Joker: 'I can see the expression on your face, what does it mean? Is it getting on your nerves? Please come and show us what the protagonist could do!'

The Bridges – a game to demonstrate the role of the Joker

In two groups. One group close their eyes, the other form pairs and make a bridge (like Tower Bridge, which opens upwards when a ship needs to go through).

The pairs have to agree three sound signals: one to attract, one as a warning and one to celebrate a successful passage.

The group with their eyes closed now move towards the bridges, which use their signals to draw them on, warn them if they are going the wrong way and congratulate them when they've gone through successfully. Depending on the number of people in the group, everybody has to go through let's say at least seven bridges.

Analogies to the Joker role

This game brings up a lot of analogies to what a Joker does. The Joker is a bridge between the audience and the scene (the stage). S/he has the function of steering the audience in a particular direction, of making sure that the discussion deals with things in depth; s/he is the Mistress/Master of ceremonies and the Guardian of the Space.

S/he fires provocative arrows into the auditorium, s/he is an expert in social acupuncture. S/he finds the right questions. Asking the right questions is when the Joker is really doing the business.

First of all it's important to make contact, to invite people to speak. Any question is good for that, for example open questions like: 'What did you have for breakfast today?' That's actually a very good question, because everybody should be capable of answering it. The simplest form of audience participation is a poll: 'How many people think breakfast is the most important meal of the day? Hands up! Why?' If people laugh that's a very good sign.

To warm up the audience or not?

Figure 29 Audience in Jangy Jer, Kyrgyzstan 2007

Do we need to do that? Again, there is no hard and fast rule. You have to decide on the spot and do what seems right and appropriate at the time. Some possibilities are: to invite people to do some movements, to sing, to ask each other questions, to take sides etc.

The most enjoyable way of warming up large groups which I've come across comes from *Cardboard Citizens*:

The actors get up on stage and the audience is invited to choose one actor to focus on. Then they have to get up and copy what the actor is doing for 30 seconds. Then you put on some crazy music for 30 seconds and the actors just let themselves go completely in all sorts of different and wacky ways. Every time I've seen it it's worked, it takes people by surprise in a very positive way and gets them energised and enlivened.

If the warm-up is taken too seriously or goes on too long it can be off-putting: if in doubt, do less!

On the content of the play

How much should we explain beforehand? I like to say: as little as possible. The play will do this job for us. Imagine that you go to a football match and the referee explains all the rules in detail before the kick-off!

Thank goodness, *Forum Theatre* is an easy kind of game. It's enough to say:

'It's not like normal theatre. We'll introduce the characters beforehand. And it's quite short. For example: this is Susanne – she's our protagonist. During the play certain things happen to her. Observe carefully what happens. If you were in Susanne's place, would you react in the same way that she does? After the play we'll ask you a few questions. You'll have time to exchange ideas about them with other people and then to change some things in the way the situation works out.'

It's better to explain less and lead people on gently. For quite a lot of people theatre is already a bit off-putting. And then to have to see the same play twice over! And then that business of going up on stage!

So we let the play do the work. A good Joker can even make something out of a play that isn't very good. But with a really good play even an inexperienced Joker can make something happen. The spectators will recognise the situation they are watching and the *Forum* can begin. Theatre can enchant: it has its own power.

If the play is being shown for the first time, leave enough time before asking the audience questions. People need time to process what they've seen.

Now is the time to think about how to build bridges between what has just affected the spectators and the important game which we are going to play. To do this properly it's necessary to get on a wave-length with what people are feeling, to sense the atmosphere in the room and then put that into words and reflect on it with everyone present. You can put a few questions which don't need answers, for example:

'Everything doesn't have to be just like it happened then. Was everything really against Susanne? Or could things have turned out differently? Where are the turning points when people could have acted differently?'

Give people time to think; a group of people is very intelligent. And make it seem easy; if you present things in a complicated way, it will really be difficult for everyone.

When you ask the first question which requires an answer, you have to be firm about getting one! 'Does the play have to end like that?' 'What do you think?'

If the group is really difficult, go back to taking a poll: 'Who thinks that the outcome we just saw was unavoidable?' 'Who thinks that there might have been other possibilities?' At the same time it's important here not to blame the protagonist, many of us would have done the same thing in that situation.

Repeat all contributions from the audience. There are several reasons for this:

So that everyone can hear them. So that you can use what has been said to illuminate something else. In order to be sure that everyone has understood what has been said.

One question leads on to the next. 'Who hasn't said anything yet?' 'Why?' Everyone should give their opinion. The Joker just collects them. We are not play-

ing the role of the facilitator here, instead we are 'difficultators'! We ask difficult questions, we challenge the audience.

'What's the problem here?' 'What is it about?' 'Do you agree?' Is it a family
problem?' 'When did things begin to go wrong?' 'What was the first moment
in the play when you thought that you would have done something different
from the protagonist?'

'Now we're going to start the play again, we'll show exactly this moment in the
scene. Then you come on stage! No stress, relax, it's fun, it's a game! And now
show us what you meant, what the protagonist could or should have done differently. When you do that, the other actors will behave in the way they think
their characters would have done on a bad day! It'll be a big challenge!'

Applause! 'How was it?' 'Was it fun?' 'Was it easy?' 'How do you feel now?'

There's no such thing as a 'bad' intervention. There are just interventions, every one is as valid as any other.

If things are getting a bit hot or time is running out or it's necessary for some
other reason, you could do a *Lightning Forum*:

Everyone who wants to change something in the play can come on stage at the
same time and stand in a line as though they were in a ticket queue. Then they
quickly take it in turns to intervene in the scene. Lots of interventions can be
shown in a short space of time.

If someone for whatever reason can't come to the stage, the actors go into the
audience! Use the moment of engagement, when there's a buzz, to get the
audience on your side. And never criticise the interventions, just use them to
start a discussion.

How do we deal with it if someone proposes a solution which involves violence?

You have to discuss this kind of thing with the audience. Usually it will very soon become clear that these suggestions will not lead to a permanent improvement of the situation, or could even make things worse for the protagonist.

To respond to the situation rapidly, you can say something like: 'Maybe for you that would be a good move at that moment, but for us it isn't. We have to do the play again tomorrow!' If someone wants to try out an intervention which includes violence, then that's possible: but only in slow-motion and maintaining a gap of a metre between the antagonists. Afterwards we can see what the audience thought about it and how you felt.

What do we do if someone wants to replace the antagonist/the oppressor in the scene?

The structure of *Forum Theatre* is predicated on solidarity with the oppressed. We want to empower them, pay attention to their situation, examine what can be done about it. What possibilities are available to them?

Nevertheless, in this instance, if you know why you are doing something you can do anything. But it must be purposeful and well-grounded. I know of two cases in which Augusto Boal agreed that it was right to allow someone to intervene in the role of the oppressor.

Once in India. When Jana Sanskriti teams are doing plays in which for example the village elders, the patriarchs, are exposed, and they themselves want to intervene and show themselves in a better light. That is allowed because it represents a kind of public promise, in front of everyone in the village, that they will amend their behaviour.

The other time in Israel: The *Combatants for Peace* use *Forum Theatre* in schools. Many young Israelis believe that if they are called up to do their National service in the Army, they will be able to be 'good' soldiers. They don't want to be oppressors.

The plays are structured so that it very quickly becomes clear that when you get an order, you don't have a choice about how you respond, and that this expectation is an illusion.

If you are not working in such exceptional circumstances, you should stick to the classic model of *Forum Theatre*: there are good reasons for it. In life the only thing you can really change is yourself, your behaviour and your attitude to things. If you do that, others in your environment will also change.

So if someone in the audience asks to take on the role of the oppressor, ask everyone: 'In real life, can you change unpleasant people that easily?'

If they say 'yes', tell them your respect for them knows no bounds!

PS:

Sometimes it happens that people want to take on roles they are not fully capable of performing, because their (sexual, racial etc.) identity is different. If they themselves know this and nevertheless want to have a go and explore what happens, then in certain circumstances that can be very interesting. On the other hand it's often the case that they aren't aware of it and then the situation gives rise to a challenge which the Joker must take up.

In *Forum Theatre* workshops in Austria it often happens that people want to take on the role of Muslim women wearing headscarves and present their situation, although no-one present is a Muslim. The debate in the media about the 'headscarf issue' made it such a hot topic that it kept on coming up.

What could we do? Our normal practice is not to talk about people who aren't present, in order not to speak for them. We make work about and take issue with topics which affect *us*. We make that clear in workshops too.

So we ask people: 'Can you really imagine what it's like?', 'Do you really know?' Often it's a case of wanting to show solidarity, but still needing to find a way of doing it.

Thinking about this kind of scene together is useful as a contribution to analysing the situation in society and one's own position in relation to it.

If for example there is a strong demand to know more about the condition of women in Islam and above all to know what the women themselves think about it, it's a good idea to try to get in contact with them, to build relationships and to invite people to workshops together. Beyond this you can also read up on the situation and begin more extensive research.

Augusto Boal described a scene from the United States. A white racist ice-cream parlour owner was happy to sell ice-cream to blacks in the quarter, but he forbade them to eat it in his parlour. Sometimes he even threatened them with a gun. In the audience there were both blacks and whites. One white spectator intervened and threw himself on the floor in front of the owner, screaming: 'If you've got a problem, then shoot me!' The black people in the audience began to laugh. The others asked 'What's up?' 'What's funny about that?' The reply came back like a bullet from a gun: 'We don't have to ask to get shot, it happens to us every day without that.'

We need to be careful about judging situations which are outside our experience (and we do so when we think we can solve other people's problems).

5. The Joker – Kuringa!

First named the *Curinga* by Augusto Boal, rendered as *Joker* in English, known as *Comodín* in Spanish, the term *Kuringa* was proposed by Bárbara Santos for international use. What's behind all these names?

The people we are talking about are practitioners of the *Theatre of the Oppressed*: they are artists as well as teachers, activists and researchers, all in one person; they are familiar with the spectrum of techniques of the TO tree and with the ethics, history and philosophy which underlie them; they are conscious of the organic structure of the methods and the dramaturgy of TO and put them into practice.

Just as no artist has ever fallen ready-made straight from heaven, Jokers don't just fall off the TO tree; and we are all unfinished beings in the process of discovering our way. At the same time that's the great thing about it: there's no end in sight. Whatever else I write here, at least that is indisputable.

Augusto Boal's theatre was developed at a time of great political pressure and so one of its key characteristics is that it permits rapid direct action for the purpose of protest, resistance, or speedy reaction to sudden developments – for a wide public, for many people who may decide to use it as a tool to create their own reality. You don't have to become a expert in order to start! *El camino se hace caminando*[55].

....
55   Antonio Machado: 'The way is made by walking.'

The Community Joker

The usual initiation into the role of Joker is to begin moderating *Forum Theatre* plays on issues you identify with and feel solidarity with.

That's the role of the so-called *Community Joker*. *Community Jokers* coordinate *Forum Theatre* groups, lead games and facilitate dialogue around crunch points with the public in their area through theatre. This work on the one hand prepares a solid base for further development and undertaking more demanding tasks, and on the other hand helps to guarantee the continuation and above all the autonomy of the work of *Forum Theatre Groups*.

The Multiplying Joker

Multiplying Jokers are those who, in addition to work with a group, lead workshops and seminars on the practical and theoretical aspects of TO; they are very solid on the ethical, political, pedagogic, aesthetic and philosophical bases; and they can sensitively fulfil all the demands which working with groups brings up.

These Jokers need to be real *Facilitators,* who make it possible to open up space in which people can learn to understand their ideas and feelings better, to analyse their problems and find alternative models of their reality. They must be able to acknowledge the multiplicity of opinions, to promote and support dialogic communication and to assist groups who have a clear idea of what areas they want to pursue, without influencing them in a manipulative way. Experienced Jokers should also be good at helping people to develop their talents and 'free up' their potential resources.

Jokers can draw on all kinds of expertise, in teaching, as actors, therapists, artists, sociologists. They have a strong sense of democracy and recognise from their own life what oppression means.

They may also be highly empathetic; they are good at engaging in dialogue and they are sensitive, hungry for knowledge and persistent.

Paulo Freire writes of the duality of teacher-learners and learner-teachers; Jokers are both of these, who tirelessly work at their multifarious knowledge and on themselves, in order to bring about concrete transformation both in their own development and in the world. An important quality of these Jokers is that that they have a 'global' identity. That's especially important because *Theatre of the Oppressed* has grown under Boal's ceaseless travelling to be a method used throughout the world, 'lived' on all continents by hundreds of practitioners and thousands of people.

Augusto Boal's vision was that TO should become a means of global transformation, and today it undoubtedly has that huge potential, so long as one is able to integrate the global dimension into one's life and work as a Joker in a specific locality.

The worldwide *Theatre of the Oppressed* network also makes it possible to extend the dialogic principle beyond communication between people, to relationships between people in different countries, groups of states, continents, and between the global South and North.

Here, where once colonialisation was the building block of what many people call the greatest wound in human history[56], which the world is still suffering from today, right here, Augusto Boal's theatre is building a bridge: it's certainly not an easy task, but it is undeniably possible. It leads from individual learning to developing projects and ideas together, through learning from each other, respectful negotiation and sensitive recognition of different points of view, to acknowledging the complexity of the task and the common work needed to create a better world.

....
56   Eduardo Galeano, Frantz Fanon etc.

The Assistant Joker

To ensure an ongoing multiplication of practitioners, in his centre in Rio Augusto Boal invested a great deal of work and effort in a pedagogy of Jokering. This took the form of workshops, seminars, conferences, discussions and much more. A good way of developing as a Joker is to accompany experienced Jokers at work and in the accompanying sessions of reflection.

Assistant Jokers can take over sections of workshops, help to coordinate groups and grow into Jokering. Multiplying is an important part of the methodology and it's always desirable and worth supporting in this way.

This also helps to ensure that TO remains the theatre of the *oppressed*, in spite of being used in so many different countries in quite different ways. But the attitude and the intention is the same everywhere – humanising humanity.

6. *Forum Theatre* in connection with Direct Action

Forum Theatre plays have the greatest effect when they are done frequently. The Indian theatre movement Jana Sanskriti probably holds the world record here, because many of its plays have already been performed many hundred times.

If you decide that you want to change something in society, in your neighbourhood, your school, your town, your country, you need a vision a strategy and good tactics. There are plenty of good examples to learn from (e.g. *Lawnmowers, Cardboard Citizens, Mind the Gap, Combatants for Peace, CTO Rio, Jana Sanskriti, Formaat*, to name but a few). For all of them *Forum Theatre* is a method, a major plank of their work, but it's embedded in a whole set of other kinds of action and activities addressing the same issues.

Everyone has to work within the means available to them. But if there is the opportunity to take an action further, don't pass it up. And when a play is ready, then it needs to be taken out, into villages, schools, into the public domain! Sending *Forum Theatre* plays out on tour is a learning experience, particularly in terms of accumulating valuable knowledge from the audience.

Interview with Sanjoy Ganguly

Sanjoy Ganguly is a founding member and Artistic Director of the Indian TO movement Jana Sanskriti, which mostly consists of agricultural workers: 50-70% of its members are women. Since 2006 all Jana Sanskriti groups, together with a number of allied mass-movement organisations, have constituted the *Indian Federation of Theatre of the Oppressed*. Jana Sanskriti celebrated its 25th anniversary in 2010 with its fourth international festival (*Muktadhara*). Sanjoy's book *Jana Sanskriti: Forum Theatre and Democracy in India* was published by Routledge in 2010: the German translation by Birgit Fritz appeared in 2011. This interview is based on questions going back to 2005, and the answers were updated by Sanjoy Ganguly in 2010.

On the essence of *Theatre of the Oppressed*

Theatre of the Oppressed to me is basically creating a space for the people to think, rationally, logically, thoughtfully and politically. We must recognise the fact that people need intellectual space like they need bread, butter and shelter. People also need democracy. In a democracy each thought can be set against another, to create a culture of debate, opposing dogma and making thought dynamic. One idea conflicts with another idea and produces knowledge. *Theatre of the Oppressed* has to be seen in this political context. Actors and spectators engage in a discussion and learn jointly.

When we approach the oppressed people we always see them at the receiving end, they are always asked to follow, by the leaders or by the organisations. So they become followers not thinkers. The idea is to transform them from blind followers to rational thinkers.

Forum Theatre for example is a collective action between actors and spectators. The theatre piece delivers a set of information about an oppression. The spectators already have some information about the problem shown in the play.

Now the information they have and the information the play offers start conflicting with each other, and that is how the *Forum* session works. People debate, propose suggestions, not in order to win against anyone but to transform the situation shown in the play. It is very important to understand this. Collective action leads to reflective action. The spectators go home and keep going over what was said, what they have heard. That inspires them to act off the stage. The spectator becomes a *'spect-activist'* and the actor becomes an *'activist'*. In *Theatre of the Oppressed* we script power and it appears on and off stage

So it is this reflection that contributes conflicts, that contributes contradiction, between good and bad, between this and that. So through these conflicts people grow. People grow intellectually, they understand the sociology of an oppression and when they are able to see the human being they have inside, they can humanise themselves. So I think this is the main essence of *Theatre of the Oppressed*.

Examples of interaction between actors and specta(c)tors

In *Theatre of the Oppressed* we want people to think as opposed to giving them advice. We don't propose a solution to any oppression. The play portrays a conflict between oppressor and oppressed, a very clear conflict. It is performed like a normal play and then it gets repeated. While repeating a scene of oppression either the Joker or the spectators stop the play and then a spect-actor replaces the protagonist character and tries out ways to liberate the oppressed character from the oppression. This is how spectators keep trying out ways to end the oppression shown in the play.

The dialogue between the oppressor character and the spectator who replaces the oppressed character brings questions out in the *Forum*. The Joker throws those questions to the spectactors. The spectators then deal with those questions and in the process, actors and spectators undertake an intellectual journey. They deal with a local problem and while dealing with it they understand the genesis of that problem. They go from effect to the cause and experience intellectual growth, I call it internal revolution, which inspires actors and spectators to go for an external revolution. Acting takes place off the stage, in real life, it takes the form of a *'theatricalisation'* of politics.

So, most importantly, *Forum Theatre* is like when you see your image in a mirror but you can get inside it. *Theatre of the Oppressed* is a mirror where you can see your reality but you are allowed to penetrate into the mirror to change the reality in the way you want. So this is how the interventions from spectactors come. And you can see variations, you can see varieties of interventions: sometimes they are complimentary, sometimes they are conflicting, contradictory. So one after another interventions come and this creates the debate. This is the first step toward a change. People debate on an issue of oppression. If you look at the development of human society, you will see the dialectical nature of it.

Theatre of the Oppressed – an institution?

No, it is not an institution, an institution will have very strict discipline and strict rules and regulations. You can call it an unorganised forum. In some places, like in my country, it has evolved as an organisation of the people. We formed *The Federation of Theatre of the Oppressed India* in 2006, and we see it as one of the greatest achievement of Jana Sanskriti, the group I belong to.

As the first exponents of TO in India, we succeeded in forming such a national-level organisation. TO is based on dialogue and democracy. Therefore you can change it, you can adapt it in the way you want. So there is no such prescription that you have to be very strict about. TO is a metaphor of social science and therefore it is changeable. What Newton said was changed by Einstein, so like that we don't say that this is the ultimate, what this is saying is: 'Well, OK, we can go ahead with the conflicts, we can change it, we can form it in the way we want, on the basis of a basic principle: and that is that we are fighting against oppressions generated by an oppressive system'.

Figure 30 Jana Sanskriti, Sima Ganguly in *Shonar Meye* – a play about dowry and forced marriage 2010

Figure 31 Jana Sanskriti, *Shonar Meye* 2010

Figure 32 Jana Sanskriti, *Shonar Meye* 2010

Main characteristics of TO in India

TO in India is suggesting a model which says that theatre, that performance in itself is not enough. Theatre is not enough, because theatre can create the situation where you can feel like changing your society. OK, so when you are feeling like changing your society, it cannot be changed through theatre only. Theatre only gives you the intellectual input, it helps you to experience internal revolution, helps you to act, offers you ways to fight oppression, inspires you to act off the stage for an external revolution. Boal used to see theatre as the rehearsal of revolution. I see it as a rehearsal for total revolution, internal and external. In India, we work with the activist movements, they are non-party political movements.

Most of them act like political parties, they send out a call, they teach people about the issue they deal with, they do a lot of propaganda in favour of the political issues they deal with. They have honest intentions, they do not work for state power like political parties, they do not go to the people for votes. In India activist movements are very strong.

Some of these movements now realise that they need to democratise their political practice. They have seen the way Jana Sanskriti, my group, use *Forum Theatre* to involve people in the political movement not as blind followers but as rational thinkers. *Forum Theatre* constructs a space for the actors and spectators to act rationally on an issue of oppression. Our spectators have their own forum in each of the villages where we perform. They come together to discuss further the issues which have been raised in *Forum Theatre* sessions. We take the same play to the same group of spectators several times in order to give them more opportunities to go into the problem in depth. I suggest you read my book *Jana Sanskriti: Forum Theatre and Democracy In India*, where I have explained in detail the need to take the same play to the same group of spectators a number of times.

Now in India *Theatre of the Oppressed* is closely connected with the world of activist movements, our group has trained their activists in *Forum Theatre*, our group Jana Sanskriti initiated the process of bringing those movements together to form the *Federation of Theatre of the Oppressed India*, now the dream of creating a Federation has come true.

There are a number of heavily foreign-funded NGOs that claim to be practitioners of TO in India, but I had better not talk about them.

Did you have problems with political parties, politicians?

Yes, see, if you understand *Theatre of the Oppressed* and if you are really a practitioner then you will have to face resistance from the political parties, because all political parties in the world, be it communist, be it non-communist, are centralised. And because they are centralised they are patriarchical. How do you understand the patriarchy? You understand it by its centralised approach. I have seen a number of women patriarchs in theatre and politics: they are highly authoritarian although they pretend to be democratic and talk against patriarchy, which is unfortunate! *Theatre of the Oppressed* originated in South America and evolved as a tool to fight dictatorship. So there is an element in the whole practice of TO that always wants to fight against authoritarianism, dictatorship and pollution in democracy.

We had to try to work in spite of the repressive nature of the ruling party in West Bengal in the past. I will not describe their practice, otherwise this will be an epic! But people love democracy, this is what they need above everything, so they supported us and we did overcome the repression of the ruling Left in our state. Now we are known, we have a big range of spectators. We reach nearly 250,000 spectators in a year through our 25 satellite teams located in different villages. Fighting against the fascist nature of the communist party in West Bengal is much easier now for us. Even so, we always have to experience vindictive attitudes from political parties in general. We are not their propagandists and therefore we are their enemy. The biggest problem we are creating for them is that we are making people rational through our theatre practice. It affects their interest as they like blind followers. This is a kind of religiosity that exists in political parties, religiosity does not necessarily exist only in institutional religion.

Where do you see the oppression in Europe?

I can talk about my feelings, my observations about European society since I have been visiting Europe regularly for the last many years. I strongly feel economic independence is an aspect of freedom; but not freedom in the complete sense. People in Europe are mostly prisoners of individualism, they are not connected with each other, civil society is almost non-existent in Europe, because they are not connected, they cannot enjoy collective power. As a result they are surrounded by a fence of fear, pessimism grabs them. They have oppressions of various kinds, the system here is very oppressive, pure democracy does not exist in Europe. But people do not feel free to talk about their oppressions. In India, particularly among the economically marginalised section, we find the existence of civil society. Unlike Europeans, they talk freely and share freely their oppressions with others. I feel those people are much less economically independent but much more free than the Europeans. In the name of liberty, people are basically accepting the slavery of market fundamentalism (not of the market) in Europe.

Generally in Europe education is more worth than experience. What is your opinion?

Education and experience are two sisters, they are identical. You need experience to be educated. In the whole world people think that university educates us, that is certainly a wrong conception which alienates us from the majority of people. This conception is the construct of the elite class of society. In my book *Jana Sanskriti: Forum Theatre and Democracy in India,* I stated from my experiences how actors and spectators in *Forum Theatre* start from analysing experience and go on to the theory. People are essentially intellectuals. We must not see it as a theoretical belief that comes from our head, it should come from our heart. Our head and heart must be connected. Otherwise we will lose the war against injustice and inequality of all kinds.

> For you it is important that the people are not only acting on stage but also in real life. How do you make sure that the process works well and the people do not just go home afterwards without drawing any conclusions for their everyday life?

We have to be meticulously careful about the process. First of all it has to be *Theatre of the Oppressed* where people who suffer from oppression are the actors. I don't disregard Theatre *for* the Oppressed. But for and of are not equal for me. *Forum Theatre* is not the demonstration of oppression, it is discussion about oppressions. We should necessarily perform *Forum* plays within a group of people who experience the very oppression shown in the play. So you see we must be careful about the fact that it has to be Theatre *of* the Oppressed and it should be performed in front of the oppressed community that understands the very oppression shown in the play.

Then what is important is what I call 'scripting the play instead of playing the script'. Here in the workshop actors become the spectators of their own reality. Thus they discover oppression. They study the ideology of the oppressor, they get to know the values dominating the oppressed characters. The play-making workshop becomes a place for cultivating social science. As a result the play-making process scripts power inside actors. They feel committed to transform their reality. Now while performing, the actors and the Joker (the moderator of the discussion between actors and spectators) should be really sincere about asking questions to the spectators. Spectators should feel the absence of hierarchy between actors and spectators which we normally experience in theatre.

No matter how many interventions come from the audience, what matters is that people are involved in the discussion in the *Forum Theatre* session. The actors need to respect their spectators sincerely, they should not pretend to be respectful to the spectators. There is no place for pretence here; what is required is a respectful attitude towards the spectators. If this happens, the actors feel connected to their spectators, the same thing happens to the spectators, they get connected with the actors and collectively act to find ways to put an end to the oppression shown in the play. It is not necessarily desirable that people should find a solution to an oppression in one *Forum Theatre* session, it is not possible also in most cases. What is desirable is that the actors and spectators discuss and debate on an issue of oppression collectively. This is how they create the foundation of the off-stage activity, which makes actors *'act-ivists'* and spect-actors *'spect-activists'*.

> Why don't people in Europe act? Why are they not happy? Is it a feeling of guilt towards the developing world?

People in Europe want to help. They think they are developed and then they have to develop the under-developed. They never question who defines development and for whom. Since 1945 a lot of development activities have been sponsored by the so-called developed states in so called under-developed countries. But nothing has changed. In India 830 million people cannot even spend 20 rupees (one third of an Euro) a day. Why are people so poor? That is the question to be dealt with. Some people in Europe think that they should help the people in 'under-developed' countries. But they don't think in terms of why should the people in under-developed nations need the help of Europeans.

The act of helping is good, but it is not enough. For example when we had the Tsunami, lots of money from Europe came. It was for a great cause. We all must be by everybody's side at times of crisis and in calamities. The time our south coast was hit by the Tsunami was considered the right moment for the then Chief Minister of Maharashtra to evict 50,000 slum dwellers from the city of Mumbai, they were evicted from their livelihood, it was like a Tsunami inland. Nobody talked about it, the developed nation states behaved as if they were blind. This is the time to be objective about the relationship between so-called developed and under-developed nation states. We should come together to act against the dehumanisation of human society. It does not matter how small we are, the global community of *Theatre of the Oppressed* should act now to humanise human society. I always feel our work has a future. I believe that *we must romanticise optimism.*

Does a dream have to be concrete? Should you know exactly what you want?

There is always connection between what you want and what you dream. If you are a dreamer, you will try to perform your dream. That's what we do in our theatre. We perform our dream, then our dream becomes performance, our performance becomes our dream. By dreaming, by performing our dreams we make a lot of dreamers among the spectators. The dream is a political construct of mind.

But there cannot be computerised formulas for how to make our dream real. The means and the ways will evolve by the intellectual participation of the actors and spectators, by act-ivist and spect-activist.

How do you see the relationship between love and protest?

In order to protest you have to have love and the feeling of oneness. From Jesus to Che Guevara everyone loved people. Jesus to me is the first political activist in this millennium after Buddha. They integrated politics and spirituality and founded the basis of equality in a complete sense. Spirituality is oneness, spirituality is love. Action against exploitation is politics. They should come together. Bruno was killed by organised religion sponsored by the oppressive state. But Bruno was essentially spiritual[57], he stood for the truth. Spirituality and science are complementary, whereas organised religion is always anti-scientific, superstitious and fanatical.

What about the caste system in India?

The caste system is a political and religious construct in India today. All political parties consider the so-called lower caste people as numbers. They are the vote banks of the parties. Shamelessly Indian capital supports the inhuman behaviour of these parties, they fund them. They also promote communalism. The most communal leader, Narendra Modi of the Bharatiya Janata Party (BJP)[58] is the darling of the Indian capitalists today.

But in trying to appear progressive we always accuse religion whereas the responsibility lies more with sponsor capital. Caste was in fact never determined by birth in the ancient Hindu tradition. Similarly communalism[59] was not the culture of India.

....

57   Giordano Bruno (1548-1600) claimed that the universe is infinite.
58   Chief Minister of Gujarat.
59   The Oxford English Dictionary defines communalism as follows: 'associated 1) with support for the autonomous rule of localized political units, such as the Paris Commune of 1871; and 2) in South Asia with the antagonistic polarization of politics between religious and ethnic groups, particularly conflict between Hindus and Muslims' (author: Alistair McMillan).

Unfortunately our education system never brought out these progressive aspect of our tradition. It has only highlighted the worst inhuman aspects of our tradition. Inhuman traditionalism and modern party politics are working hand to hand in India.

– End of Interview with Sanjoy Ganguly –

Figure 33 Sanjoy Ganguly, International Workshop Jana Sanskriti 2010

Summary: Themes Part B

Definition of oppression. Methods for creating *Forum Theatre* plays. Rehearsal strategies, jokering. Becoming the author of your own story, letting your own experiences be part of the group process, understanding that your own story needs to be seen as part of the collective history of society, discovering your own circumstances in other people's stories, being able to make connections to them, reflecting about your own society; working together to discover dramaturgical ways of finding possible solutions.

C. The Invisible Touch or Touching the Invisible

Themes Part C

Perception exercises, touch, gaze, introduction to vocal work, interacting with objects, the topic of identity, polarisations, art and its importance in peace work, the Aesthetics of the Oppressed.

The subjects discussed in this book so far are all connected, some latently, others overtly. That is the case with the various levels of awareness people have, everything that surrounds us and our knowledge of it. It is beyond my ability to name everything, and it is also unnecessary. Our friend and teacher Carlos Zatizabal, the Columbian theatre-maker, always says: 'Leave some space! Don't tell the audience everything! You won't be able to anyway.' It is the audience's task, just as the reader must do here, to take meaning from it all, or rather to give it his or her own meaning. This is an exercise in activation, but most importantly the memories, experiences and imagination of the recipients make the puzzle complete. It is through them that something new can develop, and the unimaginable becomes imaginable.

The exercises and games in this chapter touch upon awareness and creativity in the most diverse ways. For some they will be more useful than for others, offering a variety of resources that I have gathered over the years, and adopted (with permission) from my many colleagues, whom I value greatly. Who knows where they themselves 'found' them! The vast majority of them however, originate from the pool, the 'arsenal', of the *Theatre of the Oppressed.*

Augusto Boal's last book is about the 'Aesthetics of the Oppressed'. This aesthetic[60] represents the earth and the roots of the *Theatre of the Oppressed* tree. Latin American popular theatre has drawn its power from this since the

....
60   Aesthetic here is understood as an aesthetic of perception.

very beginning. Everything has more than just one meaning: words, sounds, tones, images. They are channels of aesthetic understanding. And that is a double-edged sword. Because, on the one hand they offer a means of emancipation and creative conception, but are also used as a means of manipulation. Think of Noam Chomsky and his studies of the manipulation of people by the media. And you don't need to go (back) so far.

'Who indoctrinates the imagination of our society's children?', 'Who indoctrinates that of the adults?', 'Where does this nasty business begin?', 'Where does it end?', 'The words and images in the newspapers and on the billboards, the sound on the television channel, the radio, the mainstream movie industry', 'Who decides what is beautiful, healthy, and desirable, or classified as intelligent?', 'Who gives meaning to all the concepts – which often could not be further from what they mean originally?', 'Who decides what is considered violence, and what must still be tolerated?', 'What is normality?' When you think about these questions long enough, you come to a point at which nothing can be considered self-evident, no meaning taken for granted.

If you are interested in the concrete and straightforward analysis of the influence of comic books on children and youth in the past century – from which you can extrapolate the effects of today's mass media – you can read Ariel Dorfman's essay *The Empire's Old Clothes: What the Lone Ranger, Babar, and Other Innocent Heroes, do to our minds*[61].

> They teach us, how to be successful, how we should love and shop. We learn how to forget the past and suppress thoughts of the future. Above all however, they teach us never to rebel.

....
61 Dorfman, Ariel is Argentinian/Chilean, *The Empire's Old Clothes: What the Lone Ranger, Babar, and Other Innocent Heroes, do to our minds, Durham,* Duke University Press, North Carolina 1983

I like this text, especially because it can be rephrased as follows: the *Theatre of the Oppressed* teaches us how to be successfully unsuccessful, how we can rid ourselves of our attachment to superfluous things and thus find out what love really is. We learn to remember the past and dare to think of the future. Above all it teaches us to say 'No', when what we mean is a 'Yes' to ourselves.

We need to recover and inhabit all of our creative abilities. We must learn to sew clothes once again (using second-hand material for instance), how to cook with regional foods, to find healing plants in nature, how to dance, to go on foot, to create living spaces, how to be happy without a lot of money, how to share our talents within communities and not be told on sadistic modelling shows or singing contests, whether we are winners or losers. We must learn to relate to ourselves, instead of judging ourselves harshly, as we've often been judged. And we must learn to relate to others, whom we have also learnt to judge severely.

To this Augusto Boal once said:

> It is not enough to consume culture, we must produce it. It is not enough to enjoy art, we must ourselves become artists. It is not enough to produce ideas, it is necessary to translate them into concrete and continuous social action.[62]

When we are trying to summon up our resources to do these things we come into contact with our sensitivity.

....
62 Unpublished video material, CTO-Rio.

1. The Look and its Absence

Dancing back to back, 'reading' faces – exercise for pairs

This is an exercise to build a group up, which can be done with groups who already have developed a level of trust with each another and with the work they are doing together. It is a delightful, sensuous exercise, lasting around 20 minutes.

Step 1

First the pairs dance in such a way that their backs (at least parts of their backs) are always touching, i.e. they are always in contact. The music for this exercise should be soft but lively (e.g. Rokia Traore[63]). The song should be long enough for both partners to have time to develop a shared form of movement.

When the song has come to an end, both people return their weight to their own two feet, turn towards each other and keep their eyes closed.

Step 2

Using their fingers, they then begin to 'read' their partner's face, very carefully and softly, such that they would be able to find that face again with their eyes closed. They may do this one after the other or at the same time, whichever they prefer. Give yourself time for this!

'Feel the arch of the eyebrows, the form of the cheekbones, the forehead, the hairline, the shape of the lips, the nose, the chin, where the ears begin.' 'Don't pay attention to any jewellery, but rather concentrate on the configuration of the face and its contours.' 'Once you have gathered enough information you can lower your arms to show the workshop leader that you are done.' 'Remain

....
63   Singer from Mali.

standing patiently until all the pairs have finished.' 'If you feel uncertain whether your fingers have "remembered" everything or not, you can carefully "check" the face of your partner once more.'

Step 3

The workshop leader will then separate the pairs while their eyes are still closed and move each person to a separate spot in the room. Once everyone has been shifted, the leader gives the direction: 'Find your partner!'

With their eyes still closed, the participants move around the room in search of their partner.

'When you meet another person, carefully 'read' their face but don't send them away as soon as you realise that they are not your partner. Rather, appreciate the encounter by taking time to touch.'

Once everyone has found each other, return to your 'seeing' self as follows:

'Inhale deeply. And then exhale deeply. And again inhale and exhale deeply. After the third inhalation, slowly open your eyes as you exhale and see who is standing in front of you.'

This game should be followed by extended period of reflection, first in pairs, then as a whole group.

Variation

Recognising Hands

Everyone walks around the room with their eyes closed, holding your crossed arms in front of you for protection if you like. Now, find a partner.

Stand facing each other and examine (read) each other's hands. If you are wearing jewellery or watches put them in your pockets if you can. 'What are they like?', 'Small or large?', 'Are they warm or cold?', 'Are they sweating?', 'Are they nervous?', 'Calm?', 'With or without hair?'

Once you have gathered enough information, invent a shared game: a dance with your hands, a short sequence of movement. Practise it several times.

If there is time, part from each other and continue walking in the room with closed eyes. When the workshop leader gives a signal, begin searching for your partner. 'Read' and examine the hands that you meet, and if you think you've found the right ones, try to play your shared game.

This is a kind of security-check. If it is recognised then you've found the right person. If not, you need to keep searching.

The game only ends once all the pairs have found each other.

Leading someone by a thread

The thread game is another form of leading each other with closed eyes. In it, a thread roughly 80cm long is given to each pair, who then wrap one end around their fingers. Careful: don't make a knot, it won't be so easy to undo again and the finger might become blue!

One partner leads the other, whose eyes are closed, through the room (or outside if it's warm enough), down the stairs and up again, whatever you trust yourself to do and feel comfortable with. After about 10 minutes you swop without speaking.

The only communication is the pull on the string. If the pull is not there and the tension diminishes, it is good to stand still. You can do this whenever you're not sure how to go on.

After about 20 minutes everyone meets back at the starting point and stands facing each other with their eyes open and the still taut thread between them. No one should speak yet. Now the workshop leader goes around to every pair and breaks the thread.

Then they are given the following task: 'Now that the thread is no longer there, continue playing the game for one more minute with your eyes open!' They must figure out and decide HOW on their own!

Figure 34 Workshop Kyrgyzstan 2006

The Glass Cobra or the Indian version of it: Unions

The Glass Cobra game is a variation of the many games in which the objective is to find each other again with your eyes closed.

All the players stand behind each other in a circle, with their eyes closed and their hands on the shoulders of the person in front of them. The circle can represent a snake, or else the people of a country, depending on who tells the story.

a) One legend says that during the violent conquest of the Americas, a wonderful snake made out of glass was destroyed and all the pieces were spread in every direction. Once all these pieces come together again, then the ancient peoples will rise with all their might and reclaim what is theirs.

b) In India this story is often told as follows: 'The people are told by those with political power, that they cannot be together, that they are too different. Different religions, varying ethnic origins, differing temperaments, tastes, genders etc. are said to divide them.' This artificially created fragmentation isolates people from each other and they forget the strength that lies in their solidarity and unity. Thus they lose themselves and are manipulated. The strength of the people is restored when they find their way back to each other.

Now the players should explore the shoulders and back of the head of the person in front of them, such that they could find them again with their eyes closed. Once they have gathered enough information, by touching the hair, hairline and shoulders, then they lower their arms to their sides to let the game leader know that they are finished.

Next, the leader takes each of the players to a different spot in the room and says: 'Reconstruct the circle!' With their eyes closed, moving forward slowly, the players search with their hands until the task is completed.

Figure 35 International Workshop Jana Sanskriti 2010

Figure 36 International Workshop Jana Sanskriti 2010

Seeing and Allowing Yourself To Be Seen – a very challenging exercise in pairs

This exercise originates in the realm of acting, since being seen is an essential part of the job. It is one of the most difficult exercises and thus you are simply invited to try it and then talk about it.

Choose a person with whom you have not worked very much. If that isn't possible, you can also do it with someone you already know fairly well.

The two partners stand facing each other, five to six metres apart: 'Stand on both feet, with your weight distributed equally, your arms hanging freely by your sides, without putting your hands in your pockets.'

The task is this: do nothing for 10 minutes and just be. Without wanting to portray something, just see and allow yourself to be seen. What your eyes do is up to you.

To make the exercise easier, as well as adding a further dimension, it is divided up: in the first five minutes you must do nothing at all. In the second five minutes the players have the opportunity to experiment with the distance, making it larger or smaller. But they remain on the same axis while doing so. It is important that this does not turn into a game, but remains a serious exploration of the task. Furthermore, no one is allowed to stand against a wall, everyone should still have enough space behind them to move in.

The aim is to find the distance at which both partners, on this day, at this moment, feel most comfortable.

Once the ten minutes are over, the pairs can sit down and share how this exercise was for them.

In the subsequent group reflection, you can talk about the 'Politics of Looking' in various situations, cultures, countries and periods of life.[64]

2. The Voice

Working with the voice is particularly important and enjoyable. In our daily lives, we rarely 'raise' our voice, and if we do it's rather timid. This is the result of our upbringing and our assumptions about what our neighbours will tolerate.

Because we don't breathe deeply enough, we restrict ourselves with every breath we take and do not experience our full potential. Our organs are given too little space because they are held by muscles that are no longer used to accommodating them to their full extent. This also affects our 'stance' towards life. The result is that we often giggle and squeak in moments when a deep growl or great shout would be better suited.

....
64 For example, a participant from Nigeria told me that he would never dare to look his parents in the eye when he spoke to them, while exactly that behaviour is considered disrespectful in Austrian culture – 'Look at me when I'm talking to you!' Who didn't hear this in their youth?

We are seldom, at least as adults, aware of this self-inflicted encumbrance, which we often only relax for short periods of time when it is socially 'acceptable', like during sports.

Voice work is a beautiful and resonant area of work, not only because we want to reach the audience acoustically, but also because it is our right and our joy to be aware of our full humanity and to give full reign to our voice.

Making Sounds – a few starting points

Everyone walks around the room and begins to 'shoo' chickens by making 'ksch, ksch, ksch' sounds. At the same time, we bend our knees and move our hands as though we were actually shooing a bunch of chickens into a coop.

Next we trail a bee through the air with our index finger while humming a vocal 'z'.

Then, with one hand, we hang a clothesline from one side of the room to the other. The clothesline is as long as our breath, so we must begin again if we run out of breath. While doing so, our front teeth touch our bottom lip such that we create a silent 'f'.

Next we can flick insects off our arms and legs with the explosive sounds: 'pu', 'tu', 'ku'. We can also flick them off other people's limbs.

We walk around the room and call out 'hosch', 'hop', 'hot' and then just 'hop, hop, hop', until we need to take a break.

Then we walk through the room and call out: 'You pig of a piggish pig!' While doing so, we pronounce the consonants very distinctly, move our facial muscles and gesticulate at our imaginary counterpart. The whole body should be part of the expression.

All these exercises are done for several minutes. Afterwards we form a circle.

You!

Everyone stands in a circle, relaxed, with their weight distributed evenly on both feet. The leader begins with the following words:

'You!' – pointing an accusing finger at a person in the circle. The reason for the accusation could be anything imaginable, for example: 'You ate my chocolate!'

The accused person is indignant and says: 'What? Me?'. 'Yes, you!' is the reply from the accuser and the other people in the circle, all of whom now point at the suspect. 'No, not me!' is the accused person's reaction. 'Then who?' reply the others with accompanying gestures. 'Him!' or 'Her!' the accused cries, pointing at another person in the circle. And then the game begins anew, so that everyone 'gets a shot'.

Hey, you there!

The whole group walks about in the space (often changing direction). While doing so, each person finds a specific spot on the wall to bear in mind. When the leader claps his or her hands, everyone freezes, points to their spot on the wall and shouts: 'Hey!' They hold the tension and keep pointing their finger for a few seconds. Then they continue walking.

The participants choose another spot on the wall, and remember it together with the first one. The next time the leader claps his or her hands they all freeze again, point to the first spot they chose and shout: 'Hey!', then to the second spot and shout: 'You!' Again they hold the tension and keep pointing the finger for a few seconds before continuing to walk.

They then choose a third spot on the wall, while keeping the first two in mind. When they hear the next clap they freeze once more, point their finger at the first spot and shout: 'Hey!', then at the second spot and shout: 'You!' and finally at the third spot and shout: 'There!' Thus: 'Hey, you there!!!'

When a group is all doing the same thing, it is important that it happens simultaneously, and the tension is held. Go ahead and practise it a few times. To test the effect, a volunteer can be asked to take part in a test in which he or she stands on a chair in front of a wall.

Then the entire group begins walking through the room again. When the leader claps his or her hands, everyone freezes, points to the person standing on the chair, and shouts: 'Hey, you there!', as though they had just caught them red-handed. If they are able to hold the tension well and keep the focus, the effect is quite frightening.

Sounding

Step 1 – Doing nothing with our eyes open

Figure 37 *TO Vienna*, The Twin Vision Group does nothing 2005

This exercise is very unusual. For ten minutes the whole group does nothing, meaning we do not fall asleep, we lie on the floor with our eyes open. We are simply there. And we are totally aware, not drifting off into our inner consciousness. Which is why it is important to keep our eyes open. This is a relaxing yet alert form of 'doing nothing'.

Step 2 – Feeling the vibration

After this period of time doing nothing together, we begin humming, effortlessly. We inhale, and upon exhaling, we simply send sound through our nose. In doing so we feel the vibration in our oral cavity, on our lips, in our chest, and in other parts of our body. The vibration is a positive sign of the effortlessness. So we do not want to lose it.

We imagine that the sound that we send out fills the entire room around us, from the floor on which we're lying on to the ceiling.

Step 3 – Opening our mouths

After a period of humming, we open our mouths and send a sound up to the ceiling. This does not have to sound perfectly 'clean'; as one teacher put it 'The frogs always come out first!'

Experiment with how far you can open your mouth and how this affects the sound; becoming fuller, louder, and then quieter again. Make sure that it remains unforced; you are in search of your own 'base-tone', the tone that is most comfortable for you and which is the easiest place from which you can work vocally.

Step 4 – The Sound Journey

As you walk on this journey you may close your eyes, if you like. It is important that one person with their eyes open accompanies the group and watches over what happens. This exercise begins vocally in the same way as in Step 1. First you walk carefully through the room (you may hold your crossed arms out in front of you for safety). Begin humming. After a few minutes, open your mouth and start to make a sound.

If you encounter another person and are attracted by the sound of their voice, stop and stand with him or her, and feel the vibration of their body by touching their back. Make sound together. When you've had enough, continue on your way and find other voices that attract and interest you. Move in the direction of what seems most appealing to you. If you need to, you may pause and remain on your own, just listening to the sounds around you.

This exercise is a very beautiful, but also a very intense experience. It is best for groups who have already established mutual trust and/or worked together for a longer period of time.

The exercise can remain open-ended, but be careful: sometimes it can last over an hour! The other option is to agree on a time span, e.g. 10 or 15 minutes, and at a suitable time, when it is relatively quiet, the leader begins to bring it to an end with a soft 'ssshhh'.

Afterwards, take a break and exchange your thoughts – how you felt, and how you experienced it.

Figure 38 *TO Vienna*, The Twin Vision Group 2005

Step 5 – Reflection

The voice, it is said, is a direct path to the soul and to human emotion. If we start to move with our whole body, the experiences we have stored in our bodies begin to move in us, the good ones as well as the difficult ones – our memories, and things we can no longer remember. This is quite normal. Those of us who work with theatre, even in the widest sense, are aware that in doing so we will encounter all aspects of human life.

Just like our bodies, our emotions belong to us, and we should not exclude or judge any of them when we do physical movement work. They are part of us; they are there and will eventually move on. We give them the time and space that they need.

While reflecting on the Sound Journey, it is important that you are able to let yourself experience a long silence, and to share whatever you would like to share.

Sun – Moon

This exercise offers a nice alternative to the Sound Journey, when working with groups for shorter time periods, or with younger participants.

The group sits in a circle facing outwards, such that everyone's shoulders are touching. Then they begin making sound together, that is, each person can use all the sounds found in the words SUN and MOON (in no particular order) three times. It is also fine if it is not entirely clear!

This is a beautiful exercise with which to end any workshop.

Figure 39 Sun – Moon, Sanjoy Ganguly Workshop Vienna 2005

3. Working with objects

The Human Reflection in the Garbage

Apart from the work with the *Aesthetics of the Oppressed* there are other games with objects in TO. I particularly like these activities, which Augusto Boal introduced in a workshop in Vienna some years ago, because they bring to light many previously unacknowledged perspectives and beyond that they play with aspects of ritual.

Everyone is required to bring three objects with them: they should be different and either be rubbish (but clean – rinsed out shampoo bottles, old shoes, an old saucepan etc.) or from a flea-market, so that it doesn't matter if in the end they get broken.

Step 1 – Balancing

Find a place in the room and take one of the three objects which you brought. Begin to balance it on your body, in such a way that it touches as much of the surface of your body as possible and that also as much as possible of your body's surface comes into contact with the ground. If the object falls off you, don't pick it up with your hands, but look for other ways to start the game again. After a few minutes of this, swop your object for one belonging to another person as far away from you as possible. Then balance the new object for a few minutes. Swop the new object once again with that of a third person, who once more is as far as possible away from you. Then balance this new object for a few minutes more.

At the end, keep exchanging objects with other players until you get your own object back. Take it, and with all the three objects you have brought, form a circle with the other players.

Step 2 – Images from the Objects

The group sits in a circle; each player puts their objects one by one in the middle. First, everyone places their first object, then when they have done that they place the second and lastly the third in the space.

When the objects are placed in the space, relationships between them arise spontaneously and intuitively. When all the objects have been placed, then we think about what we are seeing.

Then the task is to construct a human reflection from garbage, an image of humanity from rubbish. Everyone has the chance to shift three objects (they do not have to be one's own) in such a way that an image of a human being really does emerge. If an object has been moved, no-one else can touch it again; one can only add other objects to those that have already been placed anew.

When the image of a person, with head, bottom, arms and legs etc. is ready, it is observed and analysed. 'What is the head made of?' 'What makes up the heart?' 'What sort of person is this?' 'What gender is it?' 'What country does s/he come from?' 'Is s/he feeling well?' 'Why?' 'Why not?' 'Has s/he got hobbies? Free time? Friends?' 'What does s/he believe in?' etc.

The reflection allows all sorts of projections to arise and also lets lots of images, ideas, associations – but also other world views – become available, which the group can then consider collectively. The game ends when everyone has said as much as they want.

Then the ritual begins again from the beginning: in three rounds, each player first takes one of his/her own objects out of the picture, then the second, then the third, until all the objects are back with the person who brought them and the picture has been entirely deconstructed. It can also be fascinating to see which objects disappear first and what the last things to remain of the garbage person are.

The importance of objects for performance

Objects are always carriers of meaning and that is how we are conscious of them. When we bring objects onstage they, like all our actions, have a meaning beyond their mere functionality (as objects) and intentionality (in terms of their contribution to the action).

Think of telephones and the burden of communication in our age! It's not only that we have to be reachable and available at any moment, ready to send and receive information, but also we can be monitored and even overheard. And we carry these things around with us voluntarily, without even being certain about their long-term effects on our health! That's the world we live in and it's not always possible to opt out of it. But we can develop a kind of conscious relationship with things and use them to a degree and in such a way that they are of use to us, rather than working against us.

In TO we enjoy making visible the many meanings which objects possess in relation to the themes we are dealing with. For example we can exaggerate the dimensions or the significance of objects in our play (e.g. a gigantic papier-maché telephone which weighs down on our shoulders, or billboards which speak to us), give them capabilities and idiosyncrasies which express symbolically and metaphorically what they mean to us, how we feel about them and what we would like to change.

The critical distance created by this from what is being depicted goes back to Bertolt Brecht's concept of *Verfremdung* (Alienation or Making Strange), which aims to make it possible for spectators to see familiar things in a new light and to highlight the inherent contradictions in our reality.

4. Further exercises

The Identity Game and *Polarisations* are two techniques developed by Chen Alon[65].

The Identity Game

Everyone is their own theatre. Everybody acts and has the capacity to observe themselves in the process.

Above and beyond that, everyone has to take on so many different roles in their life, e.g. that of child, friend, worker, foreigner, patient, client, salesperson and more, so that it isn't difficult for all of us – not just 'actors' – to be able to take on different roles on stage.

....
65   Chen Alon, Combatants for Peace, Israel/Palestine

The Identity Game shows us how diverse we have to be or are in our life and also makes clear to us how many contradictions we have to confront sometimes, both inside and outside ourselves.

Step 1 – individual work

Players find a spot in the room from where they will begin their journey. They imagine it to be the place where they were born. In the course of walking around the room at length, they take a memory-trip through their life, through all the various roles which they have already played, as children, as grown-ups, as people in mid-life. They remember the roles they were cast in by society and the extent of what was expected from them, as well as roles they chose themselves (that could range from skier to rebel).

Step 2

When they have had enough time for this, they all sit down and write up all the roles which they have adopted and which they can remember, each person for him/herself. This is a personal checklist and stays private.

Step 3

When they've finished this, everyone receives four post-its. Then everyone needs to decide which are the four most important of these identities for this moment, in this group of people.

Step 4

The participants write an identity on each post-it and stick it on a part of their body which seems symbolically appropriate. Choosing the spot to stick the identity on gives them a chance to express how they feel about this identity in a different way.

Step 5

Some stools or seats are placed in the space. All the participants now walk around the space with their identity stickers on. Whenever someone sits down, everyone else stops and looks at them. The seated person then says one of their identities out loud. On hearing it, the others create an image of their reaction to this identity with their body (like a sculpture). Then the player gets up, everyone carries on walking round the room until the next person chooses to sit down. This carries on for a while.

Step 6 – in the group

Small groups of 5 or 6 people sit in a circle. They all take off their post-it stickers with their identities on and place them in the middle. They don't belong to people individually any more, they lie there discarded on the floor. Then the task is to see which of them go well together and which might generate conflict. That is the topic for a general discussion session. If desired, it could lead into developing some scenes based on the discussion.

Polarisations

In the work of *Combatants for Peace* it isn't possible to talk about just one side of the conflict, about the oppressors or the oppressed: they both exist on both sides. The *Combatants* work with so-called *testimonials*, in which individuals report what they have done in the armed conflict between Israel and Palestine.

The group is made up of men and women from Israel and Palestine who have taken part in the fighting. They've been using TO methods for some years in schools and public places.

On YouTube and at http://cfpeace.org there is extensive information about the challenging work they do.

The following way of working was taught us initially by Chen Alon in the context of our communal workshop in 2007 at the *Encuentro de Arte y Paz* in Gernika, an international conference on the importance of art in peace processes. In the *ARTiculating Values* project run by the Vienna Intercultural Centre in 2010, we used it with young people from Lebanon, Jordan, Israel, Hungary, Austria, Holland, Turkey and Denmark. On both occasions the results were surprising and exciting. A prerequisite for this technique is that all participants should be familiar with the methods of *Image Theatre*, in particular the way of making sculptures.

Step 1 – beginnings

All participants stand on one side of the room. The facilitator stands on the opposite side. The aim of the exercise is to find the theme which polarises the group most. To get this going it is necessary for one of the group to document the 'outcomes' – someone who writes down the themes and charts how they are represented in the group as well as noting the number of people on each side.

The leader asks for example: 'Who, like me, has a brother?' All the participants who also have a brother go to the side of the room the leader is on. Those for whom that isn't the case remain standing on the other side. Note: there is no 'half-way house' in this game. You have to take up a position. So if you have a half-brother, you have to choose one side or the other. It's about your perspective on the situation, there is no objective external decision mechanism. You decide where you stand, but you can't stand in the middle. Then everyone goes back to their initial positions and someone else comes up with something they want to know.

The questions can be 'weighty' or 'banal'. Some examples:

'Who, like me, is a vegetarian?'
'Who, like me, rides a bicycle?'
'Who, like me, travels by car?'
'Who, like me, was beaten up once?'
'Who, like me, gets migraine or has parents with a history of migraines?'
'Who, like me, smokes?'
etc.

This process can go on for quite a time, until 20 to 30 potential polarities have been identified. Then the list is read out and the group tries to identify the issue which creates the most division among them and which they find most interesting. This is a fascinating process, because usually we tend to look for common ground, but here we are looking directly for differences! In Gernika there was a very striking polarisation: someone stepped out of the group and asked: 'Who, like me, is a woman?' The split into men and women released a lot of energy and the resulting work was very impressive.

What stood out during the *ARTiculating Values* project was that the theme of migration polarised the young people across all countries. There was someone from almost every country with migration in their background, so there were a lot more nationalities in the room than we had first thought! One of the Dutch participants was from Surinam, a country most of the others didn't know existed. And suddenly there was a new level of solidarity and understanding, which before had not been visible (and thus not available as a resource), and which in some circumstances was stronger than more prominent conflicts of nationality.

Once the group has decided on a theme to do further work on, they move on to the next stage.

Step 2

Participants whose identity is A: sit down; and those whose identity is B: stand in front of them in a line at an appropriate distance.

Then the facilitator asks the standing B group:

'Please make an image of how you think the others see you (each one for him/herself).'

The participants do that and hold the images for a while so the others can look at them.

Then comes the instruction:

'And now make an image of how you see yourself.'

This too is observed. Then they change round and the group whose identity is B sits down and the other group stands in a row and goes through the same process.

Step 3

Now they do the same sequence again, but this time as a group. Both groups, A and B, have to make a group image to express how they think the others see them and how they see themselves. This naturally takes longer, because they have to agree as a group.

Then there is another task for each group.

'Find a third image to express what you would like to say to the others.'

All three images can then be 'dynamised', i.e. they can include a movement and a sentence, which is spoken by the whole group or by individuals, when they are touched.

An example from the Basque Country:

The women's group had created for their first image a picture of the many different faces of women in society, the whole spectrum from the academic to the Barbie doll and to the old-fashioned domesticated mother-figure. The second image was a chaotic heap of strong individual characters. The third image was a challenge to men, to take account of women's individual characteristics. Working on the images had been a longer and more difficult process for the women than for the men's group.

The men's group reached agreement swiftly. They lay on the ground and formed a large heart shape. That was their first image. The second was the same as the first, except that this time a man was standing in the centre of the heart, one finger resting pensively on his brow. The text they spoke was: 'Can I trust him?' The third image was again similar to the first and they all sang a love song.

This process can be interpreted in many ways, all of which relate in a very interesting way to the traditional image of women as victims and men as agents, which we need as a society to find ways to renegotiate and to rework together.

With the young people in Vienna the images of the young woman with an immigration background were fascinating. Their first image showed her on the ground, not knowing where to turn as a foreigner, feeling powerless. The second image produced by the group showed a whole range of different situations in which she was working hard. And the third image showed her holding hands with others and saying 'Yes, we can!'.

The last image produced by the young people without a history of migration was important – the image which had to show what they wanted to say to the others: it was an image of hands stretched right out, some of them helpful or wanting to help. The juxtaposition between 'Yes we can!' and 'We want to help you!' was the most striking moment of the whole exercise.

There might be any number of interpretations as to how this image could relate to the North-South divide. Just getting one group to allow the others to get on with it, so that each individual could work through his or her own issues, rather than always trying to join in and manipulate things, would be a big step forward.

Further possibilities: There are many possible ways of working further with these images. Each group could create a *Forum Theatre* play about how they perceive the conflict between the groups. Then they could show the plays to each other and practise interventions. These could be collected together, discussed and debated; and if everyone decided that something should be changed, they could all work out a strategy for doing that.

Communicating the human in human beings

Iwan Brioc, the third member of our team at the conference on art and peace in the Basque country to which we had been invited, particularly in order to demonstrate *Legislative Theatre*, has developed *Sensory Labyrinth Theatre*, with the goal of strengthening communities.

The structure of *Sensory Labyrinth Theatre* is an extension of Enrique Vargas's *Teatro de los Sentidos*. First you construct a labyrinth (either in an empty factory, or in a district of a city, or a cellar, or a forest etc.), then scenes are performed in it which get to the core of being human. These scenes are created in workshops in which an important structural component is the exercise *The Journey to Now*. The distinctive thing about these scenes is that they should make available to others what the performers (who are often members of the community in which this labyrinth theatre takes place) regard as important for them as a marker of being human.

Some information about this can be found on the Internet at Cynefin[66], the organisation through which Iwan Brioc carries out his projects. Here I would like to describe two exercises which seem to me to go very well with TO work.

Journey to Now

Before doing this exercise it is particularly beneficial to take a guided walk in nature with the eyes closed, and to 'understand' ('grasp') everything one comes across. Water, wood, the warmth of the sun, will all accompany us on our journey and will remain as stimuli in our memory.

Step 1

The facilitators prepare a number of large circles of utility paper (depending on the size of the group), so that everyone can sit around the room and have in front of them a nice clear paper trail leading to the centre of the circle (see Figs. 40 and 41). In the centre is a flower, or a stone, a piece of wood, a shell. The centre symbolises now, the present moment. Laid out on the paper there are paints, wax crayons, brushes, finger paints, whatever is available.

The facilitator sets the drawing journey in motion with a few words which work for him/her. Usually I say something like: 'We know how you came here, on the bus, the train, by bike and so on. But we also know that this isn't the whole story and that the real journey which has brought you here began a much longer time ago. This is an invitation to make this journey visible and share it with each other. We are not going to comment on what you show us (unless we decide as a group to do so and it seems appropriate to our pro-

....
66   www.cynefin.org.

cess), nor will we analyse it or evaluate it in any other way. The place where you are sitting is where you begin from. The centre of the circle, where the stone, the flower is, that is now. Draw your life journey to now!'

Then the drawing starts, in silence; everyone concentrates on his/her own journey. It can be accompanied by some nice music, preferably instrumental.

Alternative 1

If desired, this journey can also be organised around a theme. Sometimes I give workshops for students of the Latin American Department at the University, and then I invite them to trace out their relationship with 'Latin America'.

Alternative 2

If the environment for the group work makes it possible, you can also ask participants to look for objects and mark out the route with these. That's particularly appropriate if you are working outdoors.

Step 2

Once you have finished painting, clear away all the paints, any cushions you may have used and have everyone stand and look at their route. After one minute everyone moves one place further and again remains in front of someone else's route for one minute, before moving on to the next one. The leader can give a signal for this. The music can continue playing in the background. This process goes on until each person has returned to his or her own place.

What everyone sees will be as diverse as the people who participated. This exercise is special in that we appreciate our own path along with that of the others, share with one another what we can, and go on our own journey that nourishes the moment. The *Journey to Now* can give the seemingly self-evident the importance and meaning it truly possesses.

The Seven Loving Touches

This exercise lends itself well to groups that have been working together for a bit longer. It requires an even number of participants, who stand facing each other in an inner and an outer circle. Thus the group should also not be too small.

Each of the pairs facing one another should now find seven loving touches, with which he/she touches her/his partner. Once they have been found, the partners learn them as a choreographic sequence, meaning one must allow time for practice.

Initially we might be somewhat overwhelmed. How often do we touch outside of family or romantic relationships? But then we remember how we might have been touched as children, or perhaps we also invite our imagination and creativity to begin a loving, tactile communication with someone we may not know very well. And suddenly there are many 'touching' possibilities.

Once everyone has 'learned' her/his sequence, then we 'play' these in turn. I touch you with my touch, brushing a hair away from your forehead, you touch me with your touch, taking my hand and blowing an eyelash from my finger, and so on.

If that goes well, then there is music! And we move one step onwards to a different partner from the one we had originally. There we enter a dialogue through our touch sequences, continuing until the leader signals for us to take a step onwards to the next partner. The music, which can change continually, indicates the emotions and genre: Tango! Waltz! Exciting film score? There are no limits to your imagination.

Variation

If the group atmosphere is trusting enough, and you feel it that it is fitting, you can also try having the touch-dialogues with eyes closed. Initially with the partner with whom you first practised the dialogue, and then with the others.

Figure 40 Journey to Now, Iwan Brioc Workshop Portugal 2009

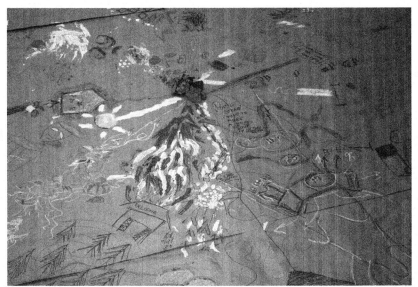

Figure 41 Journey to Now, Iwan Brioc Workshop Portugal 2009

Figure 42 Journey to Now, Iwan Brioc Workshop Portugal 2009

202

5. The Aesthetics of the Oppressed

When Augusto Boal was invited to use his theatre work to support the educational work of Paulo Freire[67], he learned to use all the languages of theatre[68] in a critical study of reality, and to make the resulting knowledge available for others. An important Freireian method that should be mentioned in connection with this is the *Picture Book of Life.*

In 2005, Augusto Boal published his essay, *The Prometheus Project,* on the international website of the *Theatre of the Oppressed*, which anticipated the *Aesthetics of the Oppressed*. The exercises suggested therein were used by the Twin Vision Performance Group in Vienna as a basis for their performance development.

The Word

Words have more than one meaning. Each word is rich with the wishes and desires of those who express them, and each receiver translates it according to her/his own structures.

For Augusto Boal, writing means being in command of the word, rather than being commanded by it. He proposes three exercises for this:

Identity Clarification

Each participant writes a few lines (half a page maximum), which are always addressed to someone else, explaining who she/he is: first to a loved one, then to a neighbour, their boss, the President of their country, the general public etc.

---

67 The ALFIN project is described in *The Theatre of the Oppressed.*
68 Augusto Boal believes all possible 'languages' are united in Theatre: word, music, painting, photography and film, movement, the sum of all imaginable forms of expression.

Poems

Each person should write a poem using their own intuition and the impulse of the moment. If this is difficult for them, you may give some helpful tips, but usually this is not necessary.

Nevertheless, the tips are as follows[69]:

a) Each participant should choose a subject that touches her/him emotionally. The emotion is necessary, but the subject can be anything from the eyes of a loved one, to the prices in the supermarket.

b) She/he should then write a whole page on the subject.

c) In the next step, the inessential words can be cut out.

d) A rhythm or rhyme can be added to create structure.

e) The last word of each sentence can be replaced by a different one which rhymes.

Texts – Describing Events

Write a text about something that particularly touched or shocked you in the last three months (or last five years etc.). Approximate length: one page.

---

69   P.S. from Augusto Boal: If you do not like these rules, make up other ones. In art, all rules are just suggestions, not imperatives.

The Image

Figure 43 Aesthetics of the Oppressed

The Photograph

Mobile phone or camera photograph of five things our hands touch daily, the goal being to choose a selection representing the individual's world. The participants should give expression to their ability to really see, rather than just look (or overlook).

What are the hands doing? The photograph becomes a heading, a title, a part of a dialogue between the world and the ways in which it can be perceived.

Reshaping the Shape

New interpretations of power symbols in our society: well-known figures, forms, using symbols such as flags, logos, coat of arms, the skyline/silhouette, the emblem of a city, things that are recognisable at a glance; the participants should create all this anew, and transform it. They can paint and draw on these, change their structure, cut parts away or add some on, can give expression to their opinions about them and to the ideas and feelings that these power symbols evoke in them and in others.

Sculpture and Painting

Building sculptures out of waste products ('clean' waste) with the theme: images of the people in our society. In small groups, the participants should build a sculpture together, showing human figures, how they work, live, love, create dialogue. There are no boundaries to the imagination. For example, I saw some truly fantastic figures of this kind at the teacher-training college in Linz. The resultant artworks are akin to the idea of playing with objects in *The Human Reflection in the Garbage.*

The Sound

Augusto Boal wrote:

> Music is the way in which people relate to the universe, it is the contact of the person with his heart and the cosmos.

This is the reason why societal powers would like to control and determine music, particularly in a commercial sense. The *Aesthetic of the Oppressed* searches for the rhythms inside us, for the rhythms of nature, of work and societal life.

Based on games like the *Image of the Hour* and others, participants choose repetitive activities from their job or daily routines, which they then transform into a dance. For this the following tips:

a) Begin by making quiet, repeatable movements, which occur mechanically in your daily life in some way or another.

b) Begin to let the movement become bigger, letting unnecessary details drop away and only bringing those to the fore which you believe to be essential.

c) Gradually transform the movement into a dance and find a rhythm to go with it.

d) Then you or someone else should create a melody for this movement.

Participants can create rhythms and melodies that draw on and develop what their body experiences when it's recharging, or perhaps, varying melodies inspired by daily life, which describe the relationship between their bodies and the world. It's important that well-known rhythms and melodies be avoided here. Tools and objects from our daily lives can be used as instruments, offering many possibilities. Depending on the time available, the theme of our work and the available resources, we may only use a few of the proposed activities, saving the entire spectrum for another time.

The results of the activities and creative processes in the *Aesthetics of the Oppressed* can be presented in (interactive) exhibits, or in public spaces, or integrated into stage sets etc. They may also be used interactively in workshops; first they are exhibited, and then the viewers are invited to respond to a piece of work that touched them in particular, using artistic means (with words, poetry, a composition, a performance etc.). The works remain anonymous if the participants request it and because temporary anonymity also allows us to 'discover' a familiar person in a new way.

The ethics of the *Theatre of the Oppressed* lie at the heart of all of these processes.

GIFT

The chameleon has given me
The gift of a thousand garbs;
The spider dies and bequeaths me
With the civil artistry of contraptions.

The tortoise dies and all of me is
Her household wealth of grays
Wisdom.
The songbird dies and my chest
Holds
A treasure trove of beaded tales.

In my clan the carver dies, I become
The forest head of gladsome craft.
I rise now the promise of brimming
Sun on my morning trail;
I rise now hand in hand with memory
Holding my frowns in fragments of
Laughter.

Figure 44 Twin Vision Performance 2005

Lost Identity

Does not want to be found again
Causes order
Chaos wanted
Immersion, going under, bathing if you like,
But not grabbing it by the head.
Allowing evasion.
A horizon of possibilities
Endured.
At least for a moment.

Figure 45 Twin Vision Performance 2005

Memories of the Twin Vision Project: two years of work by a group of almost thirty people, with participants from 14 different countries, from Africa and Europe.

Author of the *GIFT* poem is Amas Adun.

Author of the poem *Lost Identity* is anonymous.

In conclusion to Part C, here is a last exercise which is very suitable for closing a workshop weekend or a joint work sequence:

A Challenge – Making strengths visible

Step 1 – Active Listening

I often begin this exercise with the warning: this is a very difficult exercise. This is a consciously contradictory statement, since my view is that the exercise itself is not difficult at all, but that we have been brought up to believe that we will find it difficult. It should be easier to do after having worked together than at the beginning. The players are invited to sit together with a person with whom they have done relatively little, and would still like to have an exchange with.

During the exercise, each person speaks about her/his own strengths for five minutes, and then listens to the other person. It can also be extended to ten minutes. The key here is active listening. The partners may only help each other by asking thought-provoking questions when the other person begins to falter. The facilitator lets the pairs know when to switch, so that they need not keep track of time.

Surely we are capable of filling several hours time with our strengths and talents! But usually we are not used to communicating good things about ourselves. It is much more common for us to complain about our weaknesses. This exercise is intended to disengage this mechanism.

When working with school classes it can be helpful to write the strengths down on a piece of poster paper and hang it up in the classroom. Post-its can also be used, which are then stuck on the paper anonymously at the end. Visualising the positive is positive. Once the phase of active listening is finished, the next step can be taken.

Step 2 – Appreciating through symbol transference

Without speaking, one of the pair now has time to draw something, as a symbol of his/her appreciation for what s/he heard, in the palm of the other person's hand (drawing with a ball-point pen makes it easier to wash off later). It can also be drawn on a piece of paper if preferred. The drawing should express what you would like to give the other person to take with them; either because you believe they may need it, or as a symbol of thanks for sharing with you. In their hand or on the piece a paper, you send it on their way with them. In conclusion, you can discuss with each other how the experience of the exercise was.

Summary: Themes Part C

If you become more aware of your own identity, it becomes less frightening to engage with others.

Learning to have the courage to put up with differences, even over long time periods, without feeling the need to make judgements; enduring the irritation of not knowing everything, not being able to know everything; discovering the artist in yourself, expressing yourself autonomously; 'moving into occupied territory' within society; learning, observing and studying complex circumstances and situations, encountering them respectfully; remaining capable of action and decision even when momentarily disoriented.

D. Orientation: the horizon of perspectives

Themes Part D

The international *Theatre of the Oppressed* community and its principle areas of action; the 'Pedagogy and Theatre of the Oppressed' conferences; the stance of *Theatre of the Oppressed* vis-à-vis private business; peace activism; principle forms of work with and by women; *Theatre of the Oppressed* in Africa; the nucleus of all theatre work – the group.

This section of the book is enhanced by texts by Bárbara Santos, Serando Camara Baldé and an interview with Hector Aristizábal, as well as by information from a short film by *WIDE* (*Women In Development Europe*). Before I go on to explore these topics, I give a short account of one of the principles underpinning my work, transculturalism.

Introduction

From the microcosm to the macrocosm and back again. This is the trajectory that we in the *Theatre of the Oppressed* are continually traversing, which helps to bind together our analyses, reflections and activities. This chapter is an attempt to foreground some of its key junctures, with no claim to completeness, but with the aim of sketching for readers the landscape in which we operate.

1. Considerations on Transculturalism

Freely adapted from Wittgenstein: the future of the world doesn't follow a linear path.

The traditional understanding of culture has had its day, not only since the present century. The 17th-century idea that a population all behaved in the same way, that culture is the flowering of a society or a nation, has not been tenable for a long time. It is a divisive concept which is descriptively inaccurate and does justice to no-one; furthermore it is also politically dangerous, as we have learned to our cost, and prepares the ground for conflicts and wars, as Wolfgang Welsch, who has strongly influenced contemporary understandings of transculturalism, argues[70].

> The reasons for this are many and various. We live in modern, 'multicultural' societies and follow a plurality of ways and styles of living. From a social point of view we are divided vertically into different classes, and horizontally in terms of e.g. gender, sexual orientation etc. The complexity of modern cultures gives the lie to the artificial claims for homogeneity proposed by ideological traditionalists. Cultures are not self-contained units and probably never were. Cultures are for the most part invented rather than really there and this construction mostly rests on dubious intentions. (Welsch, 1997)

Welsch speaks of folk and ethnic fictions and pleads for a way of seeing things which goes beyond the polarisation of foreign and home culture. The concepts of multiculturalism and interculturalism are still tied to a traditional understanding of culture and also have a negative effect on integration projects and on the quality of life.

....
70 Essay: Wolfgang Welsch, *Die veränderte Verfassung heutiger Kulturen* ('A new understanding of culture in the contemporary world'), 1997

Multiculturalism is premised upon a juxtaposition of different cultures within the same society; it purports to signal co-existence. What results is often an attempt at 'acceptance', 'tolerance' and the avoidance of conflict, which in the long run is doomed to fail because it is still rooted in divisive thinking which crystallises difference rather than overcoming it. In the last resort, this way of seeing leads to ghettoisation and discrimination and groups are often played off against one another (as can be seen in many election campaigns in recent years).

The idea of interculturalism is based on better intentions, and aims for intercultural dialogue. Welsch however points out that as long as one retains the founding model of the classical concept of culture, which postulates the separateness of cultures, one will always be confronted by the insoluble secondary problem of the 'difficulty of co-existence and the structural inability of cultures to communicate with each other'.

We need to consider the 'interpenetration of cultures'. This includes the ability to see that, in contrast to thinking dominated by regionalistic, communalistic concepts, we can be aware both of our differences and of our intersections; transcultural sensitivity enables us to make subtle distinctions and thus to be alert to possibilities of change. We live in a mix of cultures which are interwoven to different degrees. Just as the fragmentation of knowledge has become unstoppable, the same thing has happened to humanity. That doesn't mean that we should become blind to our distinguishing characteristics. We can keep both ends of the spectrum in view at the same time.

These considerations are necessary and interesting for our TO practice and at the same time contradictory and open to challenge. Although Welsch's analysis is accurate for the greater part of the world and we are a hybrid, interwoven and mixed-up mess of people, at the same time we are faced with the dying out of languages, ethnicities, indigenous cultures and knowledges, which might move us to try to uphold diversity and maintain it to our utmost ability.

Similarly, we are marked by our geographical origins, which 'inform' our behaviour and influence our decisions; our task is to recognise this situation and be aware of it. This is particularly the case in regard to the history of oppression, as well as to its current manifestations, because in many instances these still have to be fully recorded. We should try not to bypass this recognition, this correction of the official version, as Hector Aristizábal says in his interview below: 'We must bathe in the sea of sorrow in order to heal.'

To move on from the concept of homogenous 'cultural islands' in which everyone follows the same principles and is essentially the 'same', is to open up an enormous richness of possibilities. Welsch's concept of transculturalism proposes to alter our thinking, our concept of reality, in order to start the work of integration. If we can conceive of ourselves as transcultural beings, the possibility of finding connections and of celebrating diversity grows. *Theatre of the Oppressed* in the global context offers a space to experience and live this transculturalism. At festivals we experience our specificity, alongside our points of connection, and if we can not merely cling on to our differences but consciously reflect upon them and become more familiar with them, we can grow beyond our old ways of thinking. *Theatre of the Oppressed* is transcultural theatre.

Figure 46 Jana Sanskriti, Muktadhara Festival 2006

2. The wider context of the international TO community

Theatre of the Oppressed is a worldwide non-violent artistic movement which aims for peace without passivity (see *Declaration of Principles of the Theatre of the Oppressed*, Appendix 3).

Sometimes you have to hitch the horse to the back of the cart. This seems to me one of those occasions.

Who are we? That's one of the most difficult questions in the field of TO, because it addresses one of its attributes which is both a strength and a weakness. Many people would say that we are a community which is 'resistant to organisational structures'. Is that really so? When you look at what representatives of this community have achieved and continue to achieve all over the world, you have to acknowledge that there's a good dose of organisation in all this.

A comprehensive training programme for becoming a TO practitioner does not exist. There are no institutions that could pronounce someone to be one, or revoke someone's right to do this work. There is no catalogue of groups, organisations, associations and colleagues, though such a thing was attempted for some time. It is a great, open space, somewhat reminiscent of the power of *Invisible Theatre*. Because we do actually exist!

There is a more or less loose network, with friendships born from enduring work and experiences, i.e. from of life. There is a shared love for Augusto Boal, from a generation that was lucky enough to meet him personally and become 'infected' by this work. A collective consciousness that the lives of many of us have been affected and changed in adventurous ways, that we have been granted many gifts, been encouraged and enriched. *Theatre of the Oppressed* work now exists in nearly every corner of the world. There are festivals, places where the work can be celebrated, analysed and supported, though more and more spaces are emerging in which to acknowledge transcultural conflicts and for us to grow as a result. Conferences at which the possibilities of application are examined and reflected upon, synergies with other kinds of pedagogy and art are sought for, work-models, initiatives, and movements are presented.

A globalised world has also brought many new job and research fields: peace studies, 'happiness' studies, conflict transformation, sustainability institutes etc. Ways to exercise political influence through project funding have also opened up many possibilities which would have been unthinkable some years ago. Today it is possible to find funding for nearly any project you can come up with. You just need to write it.

All of this has both up- and down-sides. Effort is too easily squandered, the surface of things is 'scratched' without reaching the depth necessary for sustainable development to occur. Nevertheless, many possibilities to gather experiences and learn from them emerge. As Sanjoy Ganguly says, experience is worth more than theory.

This results in much of what happens in the TO Community going without evaluation, as it should and must. The work changes the person doing it: *Engeki-Do*[71]. The authority that accompanies this must be your own. Asking yourself the difficult questions and exposing yourself to the criticism of the Community is also necessary.

One of our greatest weaknesses is in passing on the story of our 'tradition'. However, as we know, tradition does not mean guarding the ashes, but rather passing on the flame. The inherent nature[72] of the work helps us do this. What we are less good at, is scrutinising the experiences our past work and drawing clear, accessible conclusions from it, such that the younger generation doesn't feel it needs to reinvent everything. A lot has already been done and at the time when it was done, for various reasons, it either proved successful or not. Perhaps this will change in the future. It should be seen as very important to pass on the experiences gained to a greater extent. Then many things would be far easier to do.

There are also always new examples of use and abuse (there is actually a company which gloats about using methods from the *Theatre of the Oppressed* to 'school' their employees, most of whom work as salespeople). If parts of the method are used to reach goals other than those defined by the *Theatre of the Oppressed,* then we are not talking about the *Theatre of the Oppressed* anymore. For a while, you could find the most absurd marketing companies listed on the website www.augustoboal.com. One strategy to deal with this is not to direct any energy to the areas where these outgrowths occur; just let them wither on the vine.

....
71   See above, Apologetica
72   'To work in the spirit of', this is what we are trying to do.

2009: A turning point

Together with the CTO Rio, Augusto Boal planned the Joker Conference in Rio de Janeiro, in July 2009, before his death. It was the first of its kind. It was made up of two parts: a public international conference and a subsequent internal Practitioner Meeting.

The conference was a tribute to the cultural, pedagogical, aesthetic, political, philosophic and ethical heritage of Augusto Boal. Its goal was to analyse the influence of the *Theatre of the Oppressed* in the world.

The events were as follows:

- Panel discussion on working with TO in these areas: politics, education, mental health, oppression against women, human rights work, war and conflict areas
- Video presentations: experimental TO work in Germany, Pakistan, Canada, Mozambique, India, the UK and Brazil.
- *Forum Theatre* performances and presentations on *Legislative Theatre* by groups from Guinea-Bissau and Community groups from Sergipe, Goiás, Minas Gerais, Rio de Janeiro (various regions in Brazil)
- Exhibitions of *Aesthetics of the Oppressed* work from different Community groups in Brazil

The conference had 250 participants from 28[73] countries around the world and from 18 Brazilian provinces. 86 participants from 27 countries and 12 Brazilian provinces took part in the adjoining Practitioner Meeting (and these were only the people who were able to accept the invitation).

---

73 Australia, India, Pakistan, Palestine, Israel, Sweden, Netherlands, Austria, Germany, Great Britain, Belgium, France, Italy, Spain, Portugal, Senegal, Guinea-Bissau, Sudan, Mozambique, Angola, Canada, USA, Puerto Rico, Mexico, Chile, Argentina, Uruguay, Brazil.

The topics of the Practitioner Meeting were:

- The foundations of the *Theatre of the Oppressed*
- The training of Practitioners
- The challenges and possibilities in terms of developing the methodology
- The possibilities of stronger international collaboration

The participants' diversity of origin, their different educational backgrounds, their experiences in the field and the very different areas of work[74], were an incredible enrichment for all those present. The differences also meant that concrete outcomes were difficult to define; and that the reflection-papers[75] delivered at this conference express contradictory views and represent a kind of panorama. The most important outcome was getting to know each other, professing the wish for a continuity of exchange and dialogue and the need to develop strategies for solidarity in action[76].

There was also consensus on the need for strong regional networks and a de-mocratisation and decentralisation of the international *Theatre of the Oppressed* website – www.theatreoftheoppressed.org – which until that point had been very generously administered and made available by Formaat in Holland as a contribution to the Community as a whole.

To this end, a committee of representatives from each region of the world was set up, viz. José Carlos (Guinea-Bissau) for Africa, Brent Blair (USA) for North America and Canada, Bárbara Santos (Brazil) for Latin America, Sanjoy Ganguly (India) for Asia, Julian Boal (France) for Europe and Xris Reardon as the repre-sentative for Oceania and the nascent TO Womens' Network. The challenges

....

74 Among others: mental health, education, sexual orientation, gender, social discrimination, community work, en-vironment, violence and prisons.
75 Published at www.theatreoftheoppressed.org
76 Examples of this are the attempts in France and Austria to create an international *Friends of Jana Sanskriti Net-work*, providing financial support in emergency cases (for various groups), establishing multiplier trainings, writ-ing protest and solidarity letters, and much more.

they faced would fill several volumes. The task of writing the next chapter is ours.

That's enough about the first, really large coming-together of Jokers and practitioners in Brazil in 2009. There are regular international festivals in Croatia, Senegal, Palestine, India and other places, which are advertised on the website. Regional festivals sometimes don't advertise themselves internationally and you only get to hear of them by chance. Sweden for instance has had a festival regularly for several years.

And then there is the PTO Conference in the USA. As of 1995 the yearly *Pedagogy and Theatre of the Oppressed Conference*, established by Doug Paterson, offers a large forum for anyone interested in emancipatory pedagogy and theatre. In 1996, in the context of this conference, Augusto Boal and Paulo Freire were awarded Honorary Doctorates by the University of Nebraska. The conference, normally held over four days, includes workshops, performances, lectures, book displays, films and project presentations; it takes place in a different city each year. It is a complete world in itself, and it's worth diving into it, even if only on the internet! The regularly updated website www.ptoweb.org includes a history of the conference, details of its organising team, the previous year's programme and much inspiration.

We in Vienna have benefitted very much from close contact with another group, in our case with Jana Sanskriti – inviting them to come as visiting trainers, learning from working with them and from their work. This kind of networking most probably has the potential to bring about significant change and growth.

Figure 47 International Joker Conference 2009

3. The Situation of Women

While taking part in my first workshop with Augusto Boal (in the last century), I had the opportunity to sit opposite him during dinner afterwards. And he gave me two 'challenges'. The first: 'Stop smoking, too many people have died from that.' Doing that took me three years. The second: 'Do something for women. It's truly dreadful what they go through.' He told us about his last visit to the USA, where he spoke to the students of a professor he was friends with. He described how two thirds of the women present in the room had experienced rape; this was the norm he told us. According to our Columbian theatre colleague Carlos Zatizabal, we live in a 'culture of rape'. Patriarchy permeates every layer of society, is thoroughly internalised and embodied by women, and many men also suffer under it.

The *Theatre of the Oppressed* is a feminist movement, in the best sense of the word. My own lifetime will probably not suffice to meet Augusto Boal's second challenge; but it is a horizon against which our work must take place. Too many men and women, and above all children, as well as the environment, Gaia, our mother earth, have been harmed by this social structure.

Human rights are women's rights – Background

Nothing, arguably is as important today in the political economy of development as an adequate recognition of political, economic and social participation and leadership of women. This is indeed a crucial aspect of 'development as freedom'.[77] (Sen, 1999)

The *WIDE – Women In Development Europe* organisation is a national Austrian women's network and a central plank of *WIDE International* based in Brussels. From there they cooperate with women's organisations and networks in countries of the global South and East.

Following the street theatre they performed and actions they undertook in Vienna, as part of an event called *16 Days Against Violence Towards Women* in 2010, *WIDE* produced a short film and brought to public attention attitudes towards the situation of women in the global South, to which I will refer here. *WIDE* is an extraordinary, successful and sustainable interventionist movement connecting women worldwide.[78]

Your Profit is Our Hunger

Why address this problem here? The decision to do so was intuitive, but not arbitrary. Augusto Boal and his work in Brazil have always been connected to the *MST, Movimento dos Trabalhadores Rurias Sem Terra,* the landless farmers' movement. It is one of the largest social movements in Latin America, involving an estimated 1.5 million landless farmers. Since 2001, theatre activists,

77   Sen, Amartya, *Development as Freedom*, Oxford University Press, Oxford 1999.
78   Further information at www.wide-network.org and www.oneworld.at/wide

assisted from the beginning by Augusto Boal, have also joined them. In an obituary the movement described him as one of their own.

In India, Jana Sanskriti is likewise a land-workers' theatre movement, of which 50-70 percent are women. Thus, it is concerned with the very basis of existence.

I have chosen the subject because it is directly linked with the quality, as well as the form, of our way of life. If we become conscious of this, we will strive to play our part in changing the fundamental mechanisms in which we operate. As a result, our ability to relate to other people, women in particular, will change worldwide. It is a small step, but those who have placed one foot on this path will surely go much further.

Every-day-activism is also activism. Now it can even take place in supermarkets, or rather, in finding alternatives, such as agricultural cooperatives, organic farmers and in buying regional produce.

Further Information

According to the World Bank, 45 million hectares of land have been bought up, leased long-term, or had their lease or sale negotiated, by foreign companies, in 2010 alone. That is an area roughly the size of California. Two thirds of this land-grabbing is taking place in Africa, but other regions of the world, such as India, are also affected. However, this seemingly idle land is generally far from disused: it supports traditional forms of subsistence farming, and thus is a central survival resource for the great majority of local populations. In developing countries, women make up the majority of subsistence farmers, cultivating 60-80 percent of locally consumed food staples. Yet they hold hardly any land titles and are the first to suffer when people are driven off of the land.

Reasons for the increase of land grabbing are manifold: altered consumer behaviour, such as the increased consumption of meat, and thus the increased cultivation of exported feed crops, the cultivation of crops for bio-fuel production, as well as speculation by financiers to find new investment opportunities. Institutional investment in land, water and agricultural commodities has intensified in response to the bursting of financial sector bubbles.[79]

Slogans:

- Our Land is not for Sale: it is for People not for Profit.
- The land to those who work it.
- Land grabbing, women's rights now!
- Crops and land in women's hand!
- No speculation with people's livelihoods!

Women in particular[80] have demanded that financial players withdraw from trading in agricultural commodities, because people have a right to food and a livelihood. In order to ensure a stable price structure and the ability to plan the cultivation of agricultural resources, long-term decisions must be made, which cannot be adequately ensured by a profit-driven market.

The majority of a poor person's income is spent on food. Women and small farmers are most affected by this. A strong export orientation and free trade focus lead to a decline of regional food supplies, thus increasing dependence on imports. Moreover, land grabbing has driven many, in search of food and opportunities to earn a living, to the cities, where they must often survive in slums.

....

79 From: diestandard.at/1289608478317/Klappe-5-WIDE-Frauen-in-der-Nahrungsmittelkriese, accessed January 2011.
80 www.fian.at

Women make up the majority of those farming and keeping animals, but the control of these practices is not in their hands. In India, only ten percent of land is actually owned by women.

The women of FIAN, the *Food First Information and Action Network,* demand first and foremost, that governments stop the purchase of fertile land. Cultivatable land, in particular that of marginalised population groups, must be protected. For their part, governments should be promoting the cultivation of food staples. Women must be given land titles, and thus land rights. Worldwide, a stabilisation of raw material prices is necessary. One goal is to maintain diversified agricultural production, directed at the nourishment of the population, rather than favouring production for export and economy. Yet the liberalisation of trade policies in recent years has made it nearly impossible for many countries to protect their own agricultural markets.

Hunger is structural violence.

The endeavour to establish a women's network within the international *Theatre of the Oppressed* community

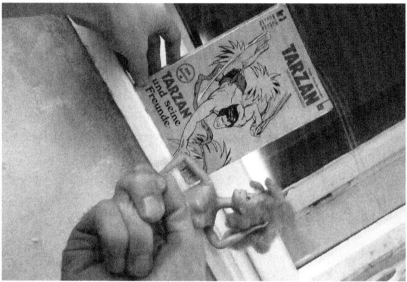

Figure 48 *TO Vienna*, gender workshop

During the 2009 'Transcultural Alliances of Solidarity' conference in Rio de Janeiro, a podium discussion addressing the oppression scenarios of women led to a collectively-drafted call for the TO Community to create its own Joker-Network for women.

A 'scene' like ours in particular necessitates self-reflective exploration of the questions: why the visibility of women in some regions is markedly less than that of men, and whether our community is prone to reproduce the same power structures which are dominant in the wider society.

Moreover, many women from various countries had the same wish to create a sort of 'women's space'; one in which to reinvent oneself and rejuvenate, but also in which to pursue in-depth research and work to strengthen women. The oppressive scenarios women see themselves exposed to engender a global bond. It is also a challenge, one which we can only meet collectively, as Julian Boal writes in his piece on oppression. This requires 'laboratories' in which to learn from one another, and in which an attitude can develop allowing sustainable change to occur within societies. Matters of gender can never be considered as separate from ethnicity, class, sexual orientation, disability, age, health and living conditions.

The goals for the women's collective were the following:

- To make the work of female Jokers visible internationally, and have a greater exchange of experience and a better flow of information amongst one another
- More publication and translations
- To ask difficult questions, rather than expect answers to emerge from the silence
- To establish a multi-dimensional dialogue about our roles in society and in the TO movement; about what it is we do, how we do it; to reflect on the specific characteristics of our placement and intersectionality[81] as women in society (health, age, ethnicity etc.), as well as how these must influence our work
- The setting up of a website for the women's network
- Finding funding for this
- Inclusivity: encouraging incorporation, alliance building, development of solidarity

....

81 Intersectionality is a term used in Women's and Gender Studies in particular (predominantly in the USA); though it concerns not only 'social gender' as opposed to 'biological gender' (sex), rather, 'gender' is merely one category among many. Further reading: Leslie McCall: 'The Complexity of Intersectionality', published in *Signs, Journal of Women in Culture and Society*, Vol. 30, No.3, 2005, p. 1771 ff.

- To use our newly gained networking power to ask difficult questions within the TO community, about the movement and its polarisations, didactic spaces, the assessment of success, and about how we deal with competition
- To determine how we may ensure that we do not replicate dehumanising practices, and how we can remain vigilant in the face of the societal and cultural structures that shape us
- Finally, the network should offer room in which we can, in a safe space, challenge ourselves and support one another when the walls seem to cave in around us (which can happen quite quickly in the precarious lifestyle of female Jokers)

All of these aspirations and ideas may not have been fully realised as yet, but the spark has been struck and passed on. Since the initial declaration, spaces for women are more frequently made within international events, such as the World *Forum Theatre* Festival in Graz, 2009, and the 25th Anniversary Festival for Jana Sanskriti in Kolkata, 2010[82].

The start has been made! Viva o Teatro das Oprimidas!

82 The complete text composed by the women's collective can be found at www.tdu-wien.at, in Portuguese and English.

Figure 49 *TO Vienna*, Her-Story, Performance Muktadhara II Festival 2006

Figure 50 *TO Vienna*, Her-Story, Performance Muktadhara II Festival 2006

Talk is good, action is better! – Spaces of women's experience in the 21st-Century

Revelación[83]

Lo supe de repente:
Hay otro.
y desde entonces duermo sólo a medias
Y ya casi no como.

No es posible vivir
Con este rostro
que es el mio verdadero
y que aún no conozco.

Rosario Castellanos (1925 – 1974)

Around 2004, Bárbara Santos and Alessandra Vannucci began the *Madalena* experiment. In the same year our *Women Only Workshops* for transcultural theatre work began at the Department of African Studies; mixed gender workshops ran parallel to these.

The workshops ensued from the wish of white women to meet black women. In the mixed gender workshops, in addition to white men and women, it was chiefly men from African countries who came, and the one or two black women, if they came at all, soon disappeared again. Feedback revealed that it was often the judgemental comments from the men that caused them to withdraw from participating in the theatre work.

The idea that there are subjects which for the most part are better addressed within exclusively women's groups, was not the primary consideration. It almost seemed as though it were 'politically incorrect' to exclude the men, leading to questions and discussion about it every year. Having a space just for

....
83 Revelation: All of a sudden I realised: there is somebody else. And since then I barely sleep and hardly eat. It is impossible to live with this countenance, which is my own and which I do not yet know.

232

women does not go unchallenged in 21st-century Europe. The explanation: 'This has nothing to do with a space AGAINST men, but merely a space FOR women' did not seem to suffice. Thankfully, the Department never questioned it.

Many women ended up in the women's workshop because they were unable to get a place in the mixed gender workshop. They then had concerns that it might not 'give' them much, without the men. At the end of every workshop I asked the students whether these workshops just for women should be offered again or not. The response was always: PLEASE CONTINUE!

Nothing fundamentally different happened in our workshops as compared to the mixed workshops. The topics, human encounter and *trans-culturality*, went through the same processes. Yet within a short time, the work developed a woman-specific depth and concentration; the questions raised were different, and a lot of energy, previously caught up in the man-woman dynamic in the mixed workshops, was released to address them. The laughter was different. Different stories were told. Many things were perceived for the first time. It was simply interesting. To experience oneself in an unfamiliar setting creates opportunities to experience things other than those already known to us. We can surprise ourselves. We can connect with other women, in solidarity, and recognise that we are not the only one with particular problems. We are able to recognise certain matters, which we may have reproached ourselves for in previous circumstances, as being conditioned by political structures. Free from shame, it is possible to speak about many things, without exposing oneself. It is peaceful and joyful, but can also be affecting, intense and revealing, questioning many things. I am a proponent of men's work, as I am of women's work, and also of a mix open to all. And I will be very happy when, in May

2011, just after this book is published[84], the first *Madalena* project will take place in Austria.

The *Madalena* Laboratories[85]

The *Theatre of the Oppressed* is committed to emancipatory work in opposition to patriarchy. Is its engagement thus also automatically feminist? Not enough, according to many women, tired of seeing the same scenarios of oppression played out in *Forum Theatre* pieces all over the world. As Bárbara Santos describes in an interview:

> When we constantly see scenes in which women are represented as dumb and helpless, we ask ourselves, what is going on? Yes, we make mistakes. Marrying the wrong person, not realising when it is time to separate, because we are also supposed to care for the family – yes, I can indeed identify with much that is portrayed here, but not with the aura of stupidity.

This irritating 'Aura of Stupidity', along with the serious questions about the 'why' behind the helpless situations represented, motivated her and her colleagues to study feminine oppression scenarios in depth. The contradiction, that women are on the one hand strong – as family sustainers, field workers etc. and nevertheless act as oppressed in society – demanded resolution.

To the great astonishment of their male colleagues, the women of the CTO Rio decided to initiate the *Madalena* project. Bárbara Santos describes how, in the beginning, she was not sure how to justify it, there was simply a feeling that it was time, that it represented a necessity. The announcement for the project made in a workshop was: The *Madalena* project is a realm of experience just for women.

....
84 This of course refers to the German edition, Stuttgart, Ibidem 2011
85 Information from conversations with Bárbara Santos, as well as her Blog.

The women came in droves. When asked why, they replied that men in society had so many spaces in which to be amongst themselves, but that women had no such spaces at their disposal. They enjoyed this exceptional circumstance.

The work began with an analysis of texts from Genesis. Eve, created after everything else had been created, the punishment at the tree of knowledge, the continuous sense of guilt, the sense of responsibility for the looming disintegration of the family, for generations. The internalised role models, the complexity of emotional, economic factors, all of these things were studied using the 'arsenal' of the *Theatre of the Oppressed*. In the end, nothing was left of the stupidity. In the meantime, Bárbara Santos has initiated *Madalena* projects, each roughly a week in length, in many countries throughout the world, wherever she is invited to do so. The participating women become multipliers for this kind of women's TO work. They use all of the *Theatre of the Oppressed* techniques – *Newspaper Theatre, Rainbow of Desire, Forum Theatre, the Aesthetics of the Oppressed,* in order to study the stance of the oppressed within the oppression, their own stance! At the end of each project week there are exhibitions, *Forum Theatre* performances, readings, collectively created paintings as well as concerts.

The workshops deal with the things that we as women have internalised: behaviours, ideas, attitudes, which open the door for oppression. The aim is not a psychoanalytical one, but rather, an intent to make the social mechanisms visible, which serve to reinforce manipulation and conditioning. *Madalena* creates a magic mirror and a creative shared space, in which each woman can recognise herself in another. In *Forum Theatre* performances, these invisible mechanisms are made visible and are woven into the production. Thus many things become visible: the exploitation of the female body, the guilt question, the matter of Adam and Eve, and abstinence. How often have we given up that which we really wanted? How often do we perform habitual actions that no longer have anything to do with ourselves?

In the *Madalena* laboratory, work with ancestral memory is also incorporated and pursued, not giving up until (at the end of the long road through exploitation and exhaustion) strength and independence, courage and the ability to forge alliances finally reveal themselves. How did it come about, that we women began to believe all this was lost? Could this circumstance have something to do with the establishment of a male god? The results were different for each location, as were the work processes. In many places the women participated in pilgrimages, and sang the song created in the theatre workshop in front of the church. In Rio de Janeiro the group of women staged a guerrilla parade, altering all 'macho' images with lipstick. In Guinea-Bissau, they took part in ceremonies for the ancestors.

In the *Madalena* projects, women from all spheres of life and with any background are invited to take part: housewives, creators of cultural wealth, artists, women who make themselves visible and want to develop an identity, women from different countries who live in the same place. The *Madalena* laboratories were also partially incorporated into the Brazilian university programme, *Minas Gerais*, and the groups continue to multiply. In 2010, *Madalena* projects took place in Germany and in India, in 2011 in Austria, and in 2012 in Berlin.

The name *Madalena* is becoming the epitome of female solidarity in their search for the 'otro modo de ser', an other way of being, as Rosario Castellanos calls it. Not only sinner or shining light, but alive, aware of her own autonomy and self-determined – in possession of her own will and power.

We are Madalena.

Figure 51 The *Rainbow of Desire*, Bárbara Santos Festival Pula 2010

Serando Camara Baldé – Guinean Women

We know that women represent the most marginalised layer of Guinean society. Normally, a woman's focus is expected to be on the domestic and private world, limited to looking after the family: husband and sons. The outside world, the public one, is the realm of men, from whom society expects an important contribution for its development. In our society, women's work is to take care of the house, their children and their husbands; if they fail to do this, they are at risk of not being considered real women.

During the last *Theatre of the Oppressed* training course, we interviewed men and women in a public market and we found that the women we interviewed were more worried about not having sons than about lacking education. It's easy to understand, because if women do not give birth to sons, husbands have the right to take another wife, with the full approval of society. On the other hand, when a woman marries a sterile man, she does not have the right to add another husband to the family; she is obliged to suffer, since maternity is highly valued on a social level and she will feel degraded if she does not have children. In many cases, she will be accused of and be blamed for her husband's sterility or impotence.

Guinean women have little space for academic development. Domestic house work, family care and working in the fields are the areas in which Guinean women are supposed to be active. Precisely because of this reality, it was of fundamental importance to hold a *Madalena* Laboratory in Guinea-Bissau. Gender work supported and gave us strength as Guinean women to seek alternatives to solve the diverse problems that we face on a day-to-day basis. The experience offered us a space to reflect and build knowledge, not only to understand oppressions but also to explore how to rebel against them in order to minimise them.

It was also extremely relevant to the issue to be able to include men in the subsequent discussion. We feel that this contributed to helping them to understand our situation better and to recognise our right to affirm that we need liberty for ourselves as Guinean women.

This experience helped us to liberate ourselves from the idea of sacrifice and to think of ourselves as decision-takers. We understand that there should be more equality between men and women; we perceive that almost everything that men do we can do too, if only we have the opportunity to do it.

In this context we staged a play entitled 'Maria – the rite of birth', based on stories told by the members of *Madalena* Laboratory GTO-Bissau. We shared stories from remote times – the traditional narratives – and recent stories from our experiences, as Guinean women in our current society. Through discussion and consensus, we chose the topic that we found most interesting: the situation of women who cannot have children so they are rejected and humiliated.

We felt very happy and satisfied with the impact that our work had within the community. We presented the play in Varela, for approximately 200 people, including the local wives of the association; in São Domingos, for about 300 people, in partnership with the regional association of wives; and in Bissau, for around 60 people. In all the places we performed, debate was intensive, and even started with women demonstrating from their seats, protesting before the play took place.

We know that there is a long way to go, but we feel more confident to go down the path.[86]

– End of text by Serando Camara Baldé (Joker of GTO-Bissau) –

....
86   Text supplied by Bárbara Santos, published in *Metaxis*, No. 6, 2010.

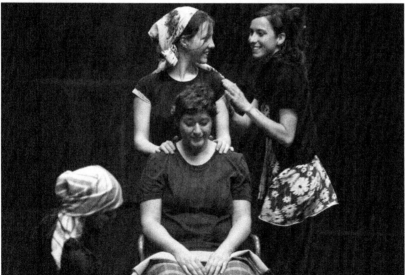

Figure 52 Festival Pula 2010 – The Transmission of Care

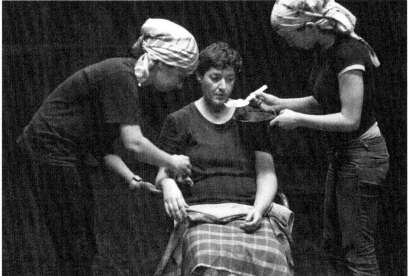

Figure 53 Festival Pula 2010 – The Transmission of Care

4. A question of position: the age of globalisation

It seems superfluous to include another text on globalisation: doesn't it lurk between every line and every page? It's part of our 'Zeitgeist', it influences every waking moment, we can't escape it. I'm sure that people graduating from high school all over the world are sick of hearing the word. 'Globalisation is the interconnectedness of all things on all levels of societal life' could be a sentence from an English textbook on the subject.

Nevertheless it's worth a few lines in the context of our work. It corrupts and 'empowers' us simultaneously. So, what now? There's not much more to be said about Nike, Coca Cola and Co. (or McDonald's), the 'Holy Trinity of global consumerism', as Gerald Faschingeder calls them. But there surely is, about what we know from the media about the mobility of goods and capital and the ever-increasing restrictions on mobility for people, at least on those from the global South moving to the North. This has turned Europe into a fortress and has brought all kinds of horrendous consequences in its wake. It seems then as though there is good and bad globalisation. The good sort has brought us easier communications, better networking, more solidarity with others, increasing knowledge; the bad sort has led to the situation, as described in a *WIDE* newsletter, where nation states no longer determine international politics, but instead it is manipulated by transnational concerns and international organisations. International regimes like monetary funds, the World Bank, the G20 and so on are growing, and a new managerial class is ascending the ladder of power over humanity, without ever having been elected. Rather than seeing this as an example of globalisation, it can be identified as an outgrowth of capitalism *per se*.

The question is not whether there are or can be good enterprises or organisations, collective enterprises owned by the workers, with the goal of benefitting humanity. They will no doubt be recognisable; and it is only natural that people should organise and work together with existing organisations. What is at stake is analysing the structures of capitalist private enterprise and the kinds of dependencies which this scenario brings with it.

Theatre of the Oppressed has to take up a position.

Figure 54 *TO Vienna*, Twin Vision, *Murro em Ponta de Faca*[87], by Augusto Boal 2006

....
87   Ramming Your Hand onto an Open Knife

Figure 55 *TO Vienna*, Twin Vision, *Murro em Ponta de Faca,* by Augusto Boal 2006

Figure 56 *TO Vienna*, Twin Vision, *Murro em Ponta de Faca,* by Augusto Boal 2006

Figure 57 *TO Vienna*, Twin Vision, *Murro em Ponta de Faca,* by Augusto Boal 2006

Bárbara Santos – *Theatre of the Oppressed* work in private enterprise – incompatabilities

Our starting point is that *Theatre of the Oppressed* belongs to the oppressed and must be done *by* the oppressed and *for* the oppressed. And it cannot be employed in the service of, or to benefit or support systems that oppress, exploit, control and manipulate, providing for a few people at the cost of the many.

Theatre of the Oppressed must be practised to humanise humanity; to enable the rebellion of the oppressed not their assimilation; to appropriate the means of cultural production instead of permitting submission to consumerism; to reveal the structure of conflict instead of smothering it by inviting ignorance; to stimulate action that demands and creates change instead of the inaction of waiting for a favour; to help to open people's eyes instead of blinding them with tricks camouflaged as solutions.

Theatre of the Oppressed must promote action in solidarity, of ethical and global dimensions, against misery, injustice, oppression, discrimination, deprivation and privatisation of natural, social and cultural resources, against land-grab and the exploitation of labour. Solidarity, ethical and international action for social justice, redistribution of goods, equal opportunities, respect for diversity, freedom of circulation, sustainability and equity of access to natural, social and cultural resources, and for the solidarity and happiness of all.

The method created by Augusto Boal is based on the *Aesthetics of the Oppressed*, which focuses on the combat against the aesthetic invasion of our brains, the domination of ideas and perceptions and the authoritarian imposition of pre-established concepts of the beautiful, the correct or the desirable. It fights against the strategies perpetrated by the oppressive system that uses aesthetic means – sound, image and word – to influence and convince the oppressed that they are incapable of creating, participating and, especially, deciding by themselves. The *Aesthetics of the Oppressed* stimulates creative and critical production of knowledge and culture in full exercise of one's freedom.

Therefore, to be practised appropriately, *Theatre of the Oppressed* needs participants to enjoy complete freedom of choice; to participate, to select the topics of their interest and to define goals and strategies of action, within the limits of their possibilities. The group needs to acquire the means of production to express its desires and its needs to transform its oppressive reality, whilst remaining aware of the challenges and risks of making them public and being determined to confront these risks.

As can be verified, the *Theatre of the Oppressed* is irreconcilable with the concentration of wealth by a minority, as well as with the exploitation of the working class, and with the banking principle of education, the uncritical or forced assimilation to a system of pre-established rules whose aim is maintenance of the *status quo*. TO is a Martial Art of open combat against the principles that support the system of exploitation.

The dissemination, maintenance and development of the ideology on which this oppressive system is based, is perpetuated by a number of social institutions, public and private, including education and research, finances, maintenance of order and protection of private property as well as communication, health, and many others including those which promote segregation[88].

Very often, as *Theatre of the Oppressed* practitioners, we work in these institutions with the conviction that we are fighting for the transformation of reality, when in fact, we are serving the maintenance of the established order. We can have our vision obfuscated and our perception prejudiced by the illusion of progress which camouflages the practical consequences of ratifying the legitimacy of the institution in question.

In a prison, for example, TO can only fulfil its objectives when the prisoners and guards are free to discuss any subject in the workshop. Obviously this possibility of expressing themselves freely depends on the Curinga's[89] skills, experience and predisposition in tackling certain issues, which in prisons are often of an ethical nature. There must be freedom to develop the aesthetic process, as well as the artistic product that comes out of this process, even if the result cannot be shared with an audience, due to internal or external limitations on the group. The aesthetic process must stand for an experience of freedom and the acquisition of the means of production.

....

88 When I refer to institutions of segregation, I am thinking of all those which have the function of segregating people, by taking them out of social 'living together' in order to protect the predominant social structure. For example psychiatric hospitals, prisons, internment centres for young people in conflict with the law. They are institutions whose priority is segregation, rather than recuperating, rather than treating or reintegrating.

89 Joker. Cf. Santos: 'Curinga... comes from a ... process that Augusto Boal developed. [...] The literal translation into English is Joker... To refer to the *Theatre of the Oppressed* expert in any language I chose to use the original terminology created by Boal in Portuguese but write it with K: Kuringa': http://kuringa-barbarasantos.blogspot.co.at/2010/08/madalena-laboratory-allesandra-v... Accessed 10/05/2012

The prison is an institution in the service of the oppressive system, a strategic institution. If the Kuringa is not aware of the internal and external contradictions which the institution poses to this work, s/he is at risk of regarding her/his work as entertainment rather than a real space for criticism or questioning, or having it turned into didactic educational theatre based on the rules in force and facilitating assimilation. Inside the penitentiary system one can only move forward in the real sense of the *Theatre of the Oppressed* when one manages to work in the absence of the contradictions imposed by the system, where there is a gap for unusual things, the unexpected, and, up to a certain extent, transformation.

The same thing could be said about TO work in schools, which in order to be adequate, requires that participation should not be compulsory and that the project does not aim to mould the students to the pedagogic model of the institution. It is fundamental that it is possible to question the power structures, so that the work is not co-opted, domesticated or turned into educational theatre. TO is not about teaching what is considered correct by a political, economic, social, cultural or intellectual elite. TO is about questioning reality, doubting the supposedly correct, stimulating reflection and building alternatives.

Many TO practitioners carry out work in psychiatric hospitals, another social sector which is historically oppressive, strategically maintaining the social order through the exclusion of those who don't fit in. In this environment it is even more difficult to protect the participants' freedom and, at the same time, to respect their thematic choices, as well as obtaining the use of spaces that guarantee the playful character of the work without it becoming purely occupational entertainment.

Although they are institutions that serve the maintenance of the oppressive system, they can offer spaces of contradiction, where working with TO can

248

create breaches of dialogue and means of transformation. At the same time, the lack of critical vision of the wider context in which the work is inserted can easily lead the practitioner into an institutional trap, which co-opts and incorporates TO, turning it into one more strategy of assimilation and maintenance of the structures and forces in power.

Developing a TO project in an adequate way, which is based on the ethical, aesthetic, pedagogical, political and philosophical principles of the method, will necessarily lead to questioning the existence of the institution. This is because the work is based on the perspective of someone who feels oppressed by the structure and by the relationships that develop inside it. The perspective of someone who desires and needs the transformation of the structure tends to question it as the central axis of the work.

And in private enterprise, where relationships are measured by economic dependence, influenced strongly by the daily struggle of workers to survive and by the explicit and overriding goal of the maintenance and growth of the profit of the stakeholders, is it possible to develop TO work, to reconcile its ethical premises and the interests of the capitalist employer?

In such a case: who commissions and contracts work? What is the motivation for this employment? Who defines the goals and objectives of work? Who defines the subject to be approached? Which audience will benefit? Is it really benefited or is it targeted? What will the actual participation of this audience be in the productive process? What degree of freedom will it have to participate? What possibility will the audience have of refusing to participate, even if it is not specifically obliged to participate? What kinds of constraint influence the decisions made by the audience? What level of institutional control does the audience perceive on its actions and suggestions? Do the suggestions of the audience represent its reflections and needs or do they try to correspond with the employer's expectations and the consequent maintenance of employment?

The capitalist's motivation is profit. This much seems clear. When a capitalist is preoccupied with the quality and development of workers' education, with attempting to reduce machismo, with prejudice and tensions in the working environment, with organic production or the reduction of global warming, s/he is focused on the growth of profit through increasing the productivity of healthy, well-behaved and happy workers or on the enlargement of the market by attracting conscientious consumers who are disposed to pay more for socially responsible and ecologically sustainable products.

The motivation of *Theatre of the Oppressed* is the transformation of oppressive realities, from the perspectives of those who feel oppressed by them.

The *Theatre of the Oppressed*'s task is to reveal the structure of the conflict and allow for the possibility of analysing the particular case as an example of the social, economic and cultural system into which it is inserted. In this way *Theatre of the Oppressed* promotes the understanding of the causes and consequences of such phenomena, which at first sight seemed particular and specific, and stimulates a collective investigation of alternative solutions. From this perspective the proper sphere of operation of *Theatre of the Oppressed* in a private enterprise would be the analysis of the inherent contradictions related to capital and work. But which capitalist in her/his right mind would invest financial resources in giving him/herself such a headache? To do shows to create awareness of the need to prevent workplace accidents, the importance of respectful relationships in the work environment, the appropriate use of tools and resources, in addition to other well-intentioned subjects is certainly praiseworthy. To call that *Theatre of the Oppressed* is absurd. In such cases, to use techniques like didactic theatre, theatre for commercial applications, Theatre-in-Education or to create some type of theatre as commodity is more appropriate, fair and ethical.

Throughout the 23 years of its existence, the Centre of The Theatre of the Oppressed, under Augusto Boal's direction, received financial support, through public channels, from Petrobras – the state-owned oil company; from Caixa Cultural and the Cultural Centre of the Banco do Brasil – the cultural arms of two state-owned banks; and from the BNDES – the national bank of economic and social development; these are the biggest investors in Brazilian culture. In none of these cases were the resources used to act within these enterprises with their respective officials. The projects developed with this financial support served to train Multipliers[90] in civil society organisations and to develop groups committed to communitarian emancipation.

At the same time, the team of the Centre of The Theatre of the Oppressed also developed projects with Petrobras' Engineers' Association questioning the directors' proposal of privatisation, during the government of Fernando Enrique Cardoso. In addition, several actions with bank employees' trade unions in Rio do Janeiro and in Minas Gerais were developed too.

As Augusto Boal said clearly on page 253 of his last book, A Estética do Opprimido, launched in September 2009 in Brazil, on the search for partnerships:

> [W]e work with peasants, never for landowners. With workers, never for their bosses. With the oppressed, never for oppressors [...] Some dishonest groups use fragments of the Method, submissively helping the oppressors: treason.

For capitalist-patrons, if they exist, who have a desire to invest in *Theatre of the Oppressed*, we have many projects committed to communitarian devel-

....
90   See Glossary at back

opment to recommend to them, where the oppressed are the ones who decide what, for whom and how things should be done.

Although financial support is vital, financing cannot supercede the revolutionary essence of our work, which seeks to emancipate and not to domesticate.

Original Translation: Carolina Echeverria; reworking by Birgit Fritz and Ralph Yarrow

– End of text by Bárbara Santos –

Figure 58 Bárbara Santos 2010

5. ArtACTivism – Collective and personal trauma, violence, healing and hope

Figure 59 Group Mandala, Alex Carrascosa Ragnarhof, 2007

The theatre, the *Theatre of the Oppressed,* is continuously searching for interstices, interfaces and cut-off points, overlaps, confrontations, looking for ways to make the invisible visible, the unheard and unheard-of heard, perceptible and understandable, or rather, tangible.

I feel
In my bones
The bones
Of those
Who once were

In me,
they are
skeletons
we are
what I am
those who were
yesterday

Maurice Rosencof, Exile and Democracy, (1993)

Figure 60 Sculpture, Zdravko Haderlap Koroška/Carinthia

BatzART!

Many years ago we were invited to a conference on art and peace in the Basque country. The Basque peace organization Gernika-Gogoratuz[91] was interested in *Legislative Theatre* and asked us to give presentations and workshops. Every year they hold conferences and also offer internships. The visit was very inspiring. Among many other impressions and unusual encounters, one in particular comes to mind. The artist Alex Carrascosa took us to Donostia to see the work of an artist initiative named *BatzART!*[92].

Figure 61 Chair circle, ArtamugarriaK Basque Country

91 www.gernikagogoratuz.org
92 batzart.blogspot.com

Figure 62 Chair circle, ArtamugarriaK Basque Country

Each month, on a specific day (e.g. on the third Friday of the month), this group drove to a politically and historically interesting place in the city. When they got there, they set up a circle of folding chairs[93], which they brought with them in their little station wagon. Then they waited. People came and sat down, and remained silent. Then a speaker came. He spoke for 15 minutes. Everyone stayed seated for a further 15 minutes, to think about what had been said. Many people had tears in their eyes. Others had their eyes closed. Most of them were getting on in years. A few younger people painted a *graffito* during this time, on a wall also erected by *BatzART!* activists.

Afterwards, the people left, the folding chairs were packed away, and everyone drove home. What had happened?

The action was just beginning at the time; Alex told us that they had begun it a few months before. They used their networks to spread the word about where

....
93   This was called 'Asamblea CreActiva'.

they would be going, so that people could be invited. The idea was to invite contemporary witnesses of a political incident each month, and hear them speak. The unheard-of thing was the act of listening itself. He added that the group would also think of ways in which to gather the reactions of the people, but that at the moment it was important and new to simply speak about things and appreciate them in the silent time afterwards.

The man that we heard speak was a representative of the relatives of the victims of the March 2004 subway bomb attacks in Madrid. His organisation had sent him into the Basque country in order to convey their solidarity and greetings to all Basque victims of the political violence. The lies about the bomb attacks, which ETA was wrongly accused of carrying out at the time, led to a change of government in Spain.

Their work made a strong impression on me. The Basque country took my hand and brought me straight back to my own country, where I grew up in a *culture of silence*[94] and fear in which the Second World War was not talked about. I began to understand what the meaning of the paralysed feeling I experienced during my childhood was, so I began reading. And I understood that I had directly assumed my mother's fear as a war-child, without knowing where it had come from or how I could face it.

One book that gave me much insight in this regard was Sabine Bode's The Forgotten Generation, the Children of War break their Silence.[95]

Theatre has the ability to create spaces in which things can be spoken about: through the performance of a letter, songs, contemporary witness testimony, old photographs and much more. Thus, it offers a space in which to counteract the forgotten, and allows *Communitas* through joint immersion in the collec-

....
94 The term *Culture of Silence* was coined by Paulo Freire.
95 Bode, Sabine, *The Forgotten Generation, the Children of War break their Silence*, Munich, Piper 2007

tive pain. The paths leading there are diverse and wonderful, because they are courageous, worthy of respect, and vital.

Figure 63 *The Labyrinth of Work Done*, Iwan Brioc Koroška/Carinthia

The following interview with Hector Aristizábal offers a few additional examples for meaningful, activist and healing interventions. It also makes the scale and extent of the realm in which we can work clearer.

> Art is the heart's explosion on the world. Music. Dance. Poetry. Art on cars, on walls, on our skins. There is probably no more powerful force for change in this uncertain and crisis-ridden world than young people and their art. It is the consciousness of the world breaking away from the strangle grip of an archaic social order. (Luis J. Rodriguez[96])

....
96   www.luisjrodriguez.com

Interview with Hector Aristizábal

On peace activism and other activist work, working with young people in the context of violence and dealing with pain as a practitioner of *Theatre of the Oppressed.*[97]

So, Hector you have been active for over twenty years in the protest movement against The School of the Americas[98]?

The School of the Americas (or the Western Hemisphere Institute for Security Cooperation [SOAS], as it has recently been renamed) is situated in the United States in Fort Benning, Georgia. They train Latin-American soldiers there. This is seen as a mark of distinction. When a soldier behaves well, he is sent to this school and trained mainly to kill insurgents. These are the same people who created the torture manuals many years ago, when the school was located in Panama, which is where it started right after the end of the Second World War in 1946.

SOAS was basically created in order to halt the spread of Communism in South America. When the dictator Omar Torrijos decreed that the school would no longer be in Panama, it was transferred to Fort Benning, Georgia. I call it the oldest terrorist training camp in the world. Because what they train is terrorists. The movement called School of the Americas Watch has documented that more than a hundred and twenty ex-graduates of the school have been linked to massacres in South America and Central America. And at least four of them became Latin-American dictators themselves.

Hugo Banzer in Bolivia, General Torrijos and Manuel Noriega in Panama are among the best-known. The coup d'état staged recently in Honduras was led by School of the Americas graduates; four of the seven killers of Monseñor

....
97   Interview conducted in Vienna in Autumn 2010.
98   www.soaw.org; en.wikipedia.org/wiki/Western_Hemisphere_Institute_for_Security_Cooperation

Romero were trained there; 700 people were massacred in the village of El Mozote and 17 of the soldiers involved were linked to the School of the Americas; and the 'Plan Colombia'[99] first saw the light of day there.

The list goes on, and in the year 2000 the evidence became so overwhelming that Congress closed the School under the pressure of the protest movement. And then they reopened it in January of 2001 under a new name, the Western Hemisphere Institute for Security Cooperation. But it is the same School with the same curriculum, they just added a few human rights classes. So that is why we, as a protest movement, didn't bother to change our name: it's the same School.

20 years after the massacre of the 6 Jesuit priests in San Salvador, Father Roy Bourgeois, who had been a soldier in Vietnam, began actively denouncing the war. At that time he trained as a priest and was sent to Bolivia to work with the poor. There he was tortured under Hugo Banzer and discovered that his torturers had been trained in the United States. So he returned to the States and the Church sent him to Guatemala to keep him quiet; but then he saw what was happening in El Salvador and when the Jesuits were killed he came back to the USA and rented a small apartment, right across from the School where these people were being trained. There he started this movement, called the School of the Americas Watch. He really did just sit there and observe what they were doing, and in this way he set in motion a very significant chain of action. At the beginning it was just him with two or three friends. Last year (2009) there were 20,000 of us. For me it is a site of initiation, because a lot of students, especially from Jesuit Universities, which are very strong in the United States, come there and this has made it an intergenerational movement. Antiwar campaigners from the Second World War, the older generation, and the very young, even some high school students, all come along; there are people

---

99   A highly contentious strategy evolved in collaboration with the USA which, whilst purportedly targeting the drug trade, served to undermine democracy in Colombia.

of all colours and ethnic groups; and many people bring their children. So it is a totally integrative event, and what we do collectively is to honour all the hundreds of thousands of people who were killed, tortured and 'disappeared' in Central and South America. There are lots of singers, lots of speakers inspiring resistance to current events.

What kinds of artistic input do you bring to this protest?

What I do specifically is, I come with Puppetistas, people who build giant puppets, from all over the country and then we create a pageant that we bring to the gates of the School, and we tell a story: last year it was the massacre of the Jesuit priests, the year before it was the story of Rufina Amaya, who was the only survivor of El Mozote. We showed her spirit as a giant puppet. So every year we do something that has to do with the contemporary moment, but that is also connected to the imaginary roots of the place, of the School. And then we do a giant ritual in which 20,000 people carry crosses with the names of people who have been killed, and the names are read and sung from the stage and as each name is read out, the whole multitude says 'presente'. And we put the crosses on the fence that the School has had erected to stop us getting close. Like this we remind them of the shame of what they are doing. Of the killings, the disappearances. And then with the puppets we do a return-to-life ritual, because having done the mournful ritual of lament where we remember the dead, we need then to celebrate life and our commitment to it through art and music. We dedicate ourselves to life and to stopping this murder so that no more people get killed. So that is one of the big demonstrations that I participate in, but I was also invited recently to the US Social Forum.

The World Social Forum

There we also worked with giant puppets and we performed a specific play about the resurgence of the river. The river that gave birth to Detroit, that is now underground, we brought it back to life in our play, along with the spirit of the fishes and the history of the different Native American communities, and the dances that they did to celebrate the harvest and the fishes. So we used theatre and puppets and images, to show the world as we want it to be, because what we want is the river back and rivers filled with fishes, not with pollution and toxic waste, we want a river that nourishes the people, and a river that has spirits, that people honour with dances and songs. We don't want rivers of cement that destroy nature and carry no water. So one of the puppets was a giant puppet made out of water bottles, that devoured people. That's another type of work I do, making giant things which are very colourful and attract people. They are not just message-oriented or even necessarily symbols of protest; but they inspire people to project things onto them, onto this giant puppet of the sun, or the moon, or Coyote, or grandmother or grandfather; people can see many things in them.

Tell us about ritual and connecting the past and the present and the future and the storytelling and the ritual work that you just came from.

This summer I was in the forest in Mendocino with Michael Mead, he is a mythologist storyteller from whom I learned a great deal. He often works with Luis Rodriguez, who is a poet, a survivor of heavy drug use, heroin, alcoholism and gang warfare. Literature and writing is what saved him. Mead also sometimes works with Jack Kornfield, a Buddhist monk who founded Spirit Rock and brought Buddhism to the San Francisco area.

I work with refugees from all over the world. Malidoma Somé, who is a shaman from the Dagara tribe in Burkina Faso, has inducted me into the use of ritual elements to honour the ancestors. So I try to bring that aspect of ritual into the work that I do: including my work with Theatre of the Oppressed. I think that Theatre of the Oppressed is wonderful in reminding us that theatre is a great laboratory to explore alternatives to conflict and challenges to oppressions. It is a great way to create dialogue among people; and dialogue that is not just intellectual or ideological, but dialogue that includes the body, includes movement which itself is inclusive, and in that way, I think, includes ritual. That is the connection, theatre is a ritual, or every ritual that I know is a theatrical event, and it has music, dance, characters, mythological figures, stories that are older than the people doing it, because stories are the storehouses of the wisdom of the people who were here before us.

And I am very interested in doing rituals because they are the places where communities can reinvent themselves, reimagine who they are. Remembering is not just remembering what happened in the past, but also re-membering, in the sense of putting our parts back together, which for whatever reason have been fragmented or dismembered. So it is a way to rehumanise ourselves, to recreate ourselves, and reconnect ourselves with the roots of our imagination, of the place we really come from. So ritual has these two aspects, it is a response to the here and now, and also a response to the ancestors. And to what happened here many years ago. This I think is something that has been lost in most cultures, especially in the United States, where people identify as white or black and there is no such thing as white, there is no white continent, no white culture, no white place. People come from different places. From Northern Ireland, from Switzerland, from Italy, from Spain, those are very rich cultures with unique music, sound, song, food, customs etc. So I am very interested in how to reconnect to that, and how to recreate, reinvent new rituals, based on this incredible luxury that we have now, which is being able to be with people from everywhere. From all over the world. So I don't use any specific things from a specific place, firstly because I was not initiated into that, but respectfully we try to bring as many things from as many places as we can. And there are some archetypal structures which are common to almost every ritual. So for instance I work with street gangs in this way.

Work with street gangs

Working with youth violence, trying to make sense of the senseless violence that they go through, you realise that a lot of them jump into this kind of ritual- istic behaviour as an archetypal response to being initiated into woman- or man-hood. You realise that the markings of the body, the tattooing and the piercing and the dangerous life-and-death-style that for example a drive-by shooting signifies, and the crazy drunk-driving, all signify a lack of support from society. So instead of this senseless death that doesn't initiate anyone, except into death, we try to use theatre. We take kids in the woods, we don't call it an initiation ritual but we hope that their psyche experiences it as such. And the other aspect that I am interested in is to help kids to be seen: for who they are. Because we all want to be seen. Especially when we are teenagers, when we are no longer children, but we are not yet adults, and we don't even know what being an adult means, because no one is showing us that.

Our parents aren't, the culture isn't, everybody is inauthentic, everyone is lying from the President to our father and mother. So we need to connect them to people who are living their own lives, who are their own authors: that is were real authority comes from, being the author of your own life. And that is where authenticity comes from, it's when you're living your own life. Whether you are mistaken or not, it is your life. So we create spaces for experience where the kids get a sense of that; and then we make sure this is seen by other people, especially adults. I make sure that the theatre work I do with the kids has a fi- nal product, whatever it may be, a poem – we do a recital of poetry read by the kids – or a play, or a dance or a combination of all these things. I try to com- bine all the art forms, and when they perform it the whole community, their parents, their teachers, their neighbours, come and see it. And it is beautiful when that happens. Because another thing about initiation is that you are seen as who you are. As a bringer of your gifts. Every child comes into the world bringing gifts. Bringing medicine, the Native Americans said. But they have to be seen. So during our life we are constantly going through all kinds of ordeals trying to figure out who we are, but no one sees it.

So when I work for example with kids coming out of prison, prison becomes a kind of initiatory process. Society is not doing it to initiate the kids of course, society is doing it because it is its business to incarcerate, especially when that means youth of colour, African-Americans and Latinos. But for the kids it can be a place where they get initiated into a very nasty culture.

But if you look at them as people who have paid a price, who have been through an ordeal, by being separated from their parents and from society, if you recognise that they had to go through something very difficult to survive, but they did survive, you are in a position to ask: 'what was awakened in them?' Their capacity to imagine things; their capacity to create connection; their capacity to survive. By fighting or by avoiding fights, whichever. So when they come back to society, instead of treating them as 'once a criminal always a criminal', which is what they do in the United States, we treat them as some-one who has gone through something very difficult; we call it 'someone who faced death and who shows life'. So we put necklaces round their necks that are made by monks in Tibet, with skulls, with animal bones, to remind them that death is always there. We put the necklaces round their necks and say: 'this is for someone who faced death and shows life'. Like this we welcome them back to life. We do this with prisoners, with gang members, with people who face cancer, or illnesses, or mental health problems, nervous breakdowns, things like that, so they feel seen, and they can say 'Oh, I came back!'

Do you see pain as a fundamental experience, which everyone shares and which they bring with them to theatre work, although in other situations peo-ple don't like to speak about it?

In the mix of things I am doing when I work with TO, a lot of emotional pain comes up, but we are not doing psychotherapy, although sometimes that's what people suppose we're doing... But no, there are other ways, like just singing songs, and then we all connect. There is nothing like our woundedness to create community.

Every time I do a workshop, when the pain starts showing up, immediately we are all connected, and we don't know what to do with it. When we are alone, we remain alone. When you can cry with a group, when you create a lake of sorrow, we all bathe in it. And then after that we can laugh, we all need that, we need to weep and then to be able to leave it behind.

One of the simple definitions of ritual that I like the most is that ritual is a space in which we experience what we always needed or wanted to experience but that we could not experience on our own. So when I do my performance about torture, I no longer remember my own experience but when I tell it, I share it with other people using art and they help me carry the story; and it's not only my story, it's the story of my brother's murder, the story of assassination, and of all the people who are going through that. So it is no longer my personal drama, my personal nightmare. I put it out there, and together we explore it. And we can say, OK, what do we do about this? So there is a personal healing aspect and a socio-political aspect to it. Transforming it through action. Because yes, ideology can move some of us. But most people don't get moved by ideology. And they get swamped by that other ideology, that tells us: 'What's wrong with you? You can be everything you want to be!', instead of one that says: 'You can be who you are'. And consume this and consume that, that kind of ideology... But when people connect through their wounds, it's amazing, it's an awakening. I see more and more of that for example in the USA: take the case of Cindy Sheehan. After her son was killed in Iraq, she started to ask: 'Why?' And she went to George Bush and said: 'Tell me why my son was sacrificed. Why was he killed?' And George Bush said: 'I'm sorry Ma'am, but I don't have an answer'. And she said: 'No, you have to give me an answer'; and she just persisted and the man went crazy and said: 'I'm going to Texas, I'm on vacation'. And she went and put a tent in front of his ranch in Texas and very soon ten thousand people showed up. She didn't call those ten thousand people. But a lot of us activists and a lot of us mothers and fathers said, she is asking the question I want to ask. So they came. So she became a vessel for something that is there in the culture. But it took the readiness to open herself to her wound, to the horrible hole that she felt when they came to tell her – when they knocked on her door and said: 'Ma'am, we are so sorry to inform you that your son has been killed in the course of duty.' And when she talks about that, she says, my heart was torn out. But then, through that hole came the thought: 'Wait a minute, I can do something, for some other people's sons and daughters.' That happens over and over.

I always hope that people don't need to get wounded that way in order to wake up.

– End of the interview with Hector Aristizábal –

Figure 64 Hector Aristizábal 2010

6. Beginning at the end

The nucleus – the theatre group

Never doubt that a small group of thoughtful, committed people can change the world. Indeed, it is the only thing that ever has. (Margaret Mead)

The engine of theatre work is the group. Second or first family, Utopia experienced for real, experimental and laboratory space, home, theatre movement or collective... the multiplication of *Theatre of the Oppressed* has been driven by inspiring new groups to form, because 'togetherness is strength' and 'our story isn't just ours, it's everyone's'. Knowing that is already a big step.

Groups come together as a result of living through situations with others, from similar visions, capacities, protests or artistic ambitions, which are underpinned by the desire for change which begins in the individual and his/her environment.

Latin America, the birthplace of the *Theatre of the Oppressed*, has a long tradition of politically-inspired theatre groups, which were also, in times of great repression and statist violence, places of collective strength – as they are still. Literature on this is listed in the Bibliography and available in libraries and on the web. Two of the most important Columbian theatre groups, TEC (*Teatro Experimental de Cali*), with its founder Enrique Buenaventura, and *La Candelaria,* with Santiago Garcia, represent an important chapter in Latin-American theatre history. The method of *Collective Creation,* which they use as the basis for creating plays, is also one of the roots of TO and its journey towards *Forum Theatre.*

In Brazil as well as Columbia, theatre groups decided to adopt a model from agricultural collectives for their own purposes, that is to say, a cooperative structure. The *Cooperativa Paulista do Teatro* brings together about 1000 theatre groups in Sao Paulo alone. The *Cooperativa Colombiano de Teatro* is both a Columbian theatre group and a platform which organises a yearly Open Stage Festival. These coming-togethers are (like many festivals) important networking occasions where people can meet and draw strength from each other, which helps significantly to inspire new and positive change.

In the book *Techniques of Popular Latin-American Theatre* (1975)[100], Augusto Boal describes the Latin-American folk theatre movements and initiatives and gives a list of the important theatre groups at that time. Many of them still exist, albeit in modified form.

It seems to be easier to come together in this way in India and in many Latin-American countries; in Europe however we seem to be scared of our own shadows. Whether it is a stronger sense of individual identity, or an excess of opportunities for engagement, or lack of trust, or the fear of missing out on something which is happening somewhere else, or a reluctance to let oneself be pinned down – or perhaps a combination of all of these – the result is that theatre groups tend to remain time-bound endeavours, to be avenues for paid work, or to function as spare-time activities for amusement rather than anything requiring ongoing commitment. In spite of this, they can and do often provide important kinds of experience and mark important stages of people's lives.

At the *World Festival of Forum Theatre* in Austria (2009) and the 25th anniversary of Jana Sanskriti in Kolkata (2010), it was possible to sense a growth in the number of young TO theatre groups. And there are also a few groups which have been in existence for quite a long time, which provide very inspirational

....
100 Original text written in Spanish: Boal, Augusto, *Técnicas Latinoamericanas de Teatro Popular, Una revolución copernicana al revés*, Ediciones Corregidor, Buenos Aires 1975

models to follow. I will mention one such group from the German-speaking area.

ATG-Halle – an unusual example of an experimental European theatre group

Supplementary Note

Aktionstheatergruppe (ATG) Halle has been in existence since April 2002 and is an open theatre group with 10-15 members from differing educational and professional backgrounds. Following an initial period of development work on the DOMINO Project – championing civil rights – in collaboration with two experienced theatre trainers[101], the group established its own independent agenda from 2004. It mostly uses Boal's TO methodology and creates street performance events which animate market places and shopping zones. They also go into schools and prisons, perform at day conferences on specific topics, or in public spaces, presenting Forum plays on themes like exclusion, isolation, violence in the family, racism and sexism. At the centre of the work is collective development and construction of scenes and of the ensuing interactive dialogue with the audience.

Their performances and plays arise from individuals' interest in current conflicts and problems. The goal is to raise questions, open eyes, to incite thought and action. They use blue plastic barrels as percussion instruments, décor and props. Since 2005 they have been giving theatre workshops in schools, based on TO methods[102].

....
101 Katrin Wolf and Till Baumann
102 Taken from the official text of the World Forum Theatre Festival in Austria, 2009

Figure 65 Giant puppets by ATG-Halle and Jana Sanskriti, Muktadhara IV Festival 2010

Figure 66 Giant puppets by ATG-Halle and Jana Sanskriti, Muktadhara IV Festival 2010

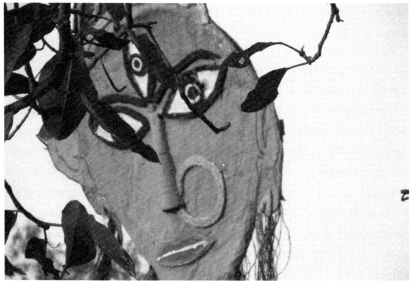

Figure 67 Giant puppets by ATG-Halle and Jana Sanskriti, Muktadhara IV Festival 2010

WHEREVER ATG POPS UP THERE ARE GIANT PUPPETS AND VIBRANT BRAZILI-AN-INSPIRED SAMBA DRUMMING ON BIG BLUE PLASTIC BARRELS.

The story began one year with the planning of the 16th June anniversary of the alternative autonomous cultural centre at 78 Reilstrasse in Halle, which the group used and helped to energise. Then news came about the annual Nazi parade on June 17th[103], which had been officially announced and sanctioned. Its use of banners and placards like 'No German money for foreign interests' was enough to spark a creative response. The members of ATG set up 'Re-creaction Picnic Days' and took responsibility for devising and organising them. Marc Amann, author of the book *Go, Stop, Act!*, and Till Baumann were invited to be animators. Amann assisted the group with making giant puppets and

....

103 Background: on June 17th 1953 in the DDR (East German Republic), the so-called workers' revolt took place. The Halle-Bitterfeld area was one of the centres of the protest. For several years the Neo-Nazis have been trying to claim this date for themselves. For example, in 2009, the Saxony leadership of the Neo-Nazis called for a demonstration in Halle.

Baumann contributed lively Samba rhythms for the street events. All this was woven into a collaborative choreography.

The cultural centre's anniversary celebration became a dress rehearsal for the counter-demonstration. The latter was a total success. It was colourful, joyous and positive and in this way the group made it possible for lots of people to join the theatre protest activities spontaneously. It created a good mood, and it halted the right-wing procession: the Nazis were unable to reach their goal. This action became a trailblazer. Given the large number of Nazi parades in Germany, ATG had plenty of opportunity to repeat it and to organise workshops in the interim; they were also able to spread the idea of using plastic barrels for percussion and to network with other groups and organisations. As a result, one particular group came into being with the purpose of devoting itself specifically to the issue of 'activism against the far right'. Prior to scheduled events, many people – sometimes as many as 50 – came together for a weekend to spruce up the puppets and make new ones, to work out choreographies and methods of communication for use during the action. The aim is consensus, the path creates the goal. It is fascinating how quickly people begin to get on well with each other when they are involved in having fun making meaning through creativity, group collaboration and music; people who hadn't even taken part in a demonstration before, who for various reasons hadn't wanted or been able to commit themselves, or who had been scared off by the loud voices on demonstrations, the anger, the frustration, by things they didn't want to be part of. Attracted by the artistic elements, people began to take part in discussions about socio-political action and participation. For ATG, the experience of reaching people from 'outside' through their work was very salutary. In addition, the creative intervention of ATG usually shifted the mood of the political events: for instance, if it was very cold and there was a lot of sitting and waiting, people felt a need to dance and so they did that, instead of throwing snowballs at the police. In Dresden, where the biggest Nazi parade in Europe had taken place for many years in February, ATG was one of several activist groups who decided to oppose it. This kind of activist consensus signals freedom from violence, but with a specific mode of response which is manifested through extensive bodily, visual and acoustic presence and by not letting oneself be intimidated.

Another unusual theatre event ATG was involved in was like a radio ballet[104], which took place in the context of an action connected with the 'memory train'[105]. After refusing for years to accommodate the acts of remembrance for the children deported and murdered in the Second World War, the German Railways agreed that a hired train carrying an exhibition could use their network and enlighten people about the history of their local stations.

The group distances itself expressly from the *Creative Resistance Movement* and the *Rebel Clown Army* from the UK[106]. ATG did make contact with them and attended some workshops, as well as exploring some forms of creative resistance for themselves, but they were clear that they took a different position. The characterisation of the army and the police by the UK groups was too crude; and making fun of state authority would not go down well in Germany. Moreover, keeping a piece of theatre going for three hours without a break from playing the role of clowns seemed likely to be too exhausting, and ultimately to compromise the very idea which the clown represents.

....
104 de.wikipedia.org/wiki/Radioballett
105 www.zugdererinnerung.de
106 See http://www.rebelclown.net/clog

EVERY STANDPOINT AND EVERY CONTEXT REQUIRES ITS OWN FORM OF TRANSFORMATIONAL THEATRE!

Group atmospherics and international networking – external contacts

In 2004 the first members of ATG began to go to India to Jana Sanskriti's festivals[107]. In 2006 they organised a clown workshop with the Spanish/Catalan teacher David Martinez in Finland. This workshop was advertised to the whole international TO network and received no external sponsorship. People paid their own travel costs and everyone put in 50 euros to the group kitty; all work in the workshop location, a small farm in the country, from building toilets to cooking, was shared; a few sympathisers came along too in order to lend a hand without taking part in the theatre work. Working for the collective in this way strengthened the group greatly, it was a great example of what working together can achieve. The vision of creating a more permanent collective comes to the surface every now and then and then fades. Further workshops were organised to which Sanjoy Ganguly, Hector Aristizábal and Bárbara Santos were invited; offers and invitations were extended throughout the region to people in and around Halle, to people on the artistic scene and to international contacts; the network was growing.

The autonomous culture centre at Reilstrasse 78[108] likewise contributes a great deal to the group dynamic and the group consciousness. There is no rent charged to users but people contribute in other ways: sometimes by paying for specific items, by helping with the Christmas clean-up, or by collecting wood for heating, doing bar and repair work and so on. Active participation and communal work strengthen and influence the theatre group; they influence both the resulting theatre work and the way in which the group functions in and for itself and within the community, and have a direct impact on life and work in the 'real' world.

....
107 Muktadhara International Theatre of the Oppressed Festivals 1-4 (2004, 2006, 2008, 2010)
108 www.reil78.de

THE WAY A THEATRE GROUP IS EMBEDDED IN THE LOCALITY DETERMINES THE SCOPE OF ACTIVITY AND THE QUALITY OF THE WORK

Leadership, democracy and organisational issues

At first, four members who had been fully trained took it in turns to lead projects; after about a year this was amended so that another group member assisted on each project and sequence of rehearsals, in order to develop the capacity to direct and to take the role of Joker. That was an important step in the democratisation of the group. This alternation of responsibilities parallels the ethos of collective creation and gives everyone the chance to develop new and important skills. Other responsibilities (finance, administration) are likewise rotated. Alongside this, for each new project the roles are agreed and allocated well in advance, including not only direction but also initial research and other key phases.

A major decision was that, in order to maintain freedom, ATG should not become a professional organisation accepting work on a commission basis. An organisational structure, *Aktionstheater Halle e.V. (ATH e.V.)* was formed in order to allow those members who so desire to design projects and offer workshops, e.g. in schools: members have to signal whether they want to do this or not, and the activities of the two groups remain separate.

MEMBERS' INDIVIDUAL NEEDS MUST BE ACKNOWLEDGED AND ACCOMMODATED

Impact on personal life

The impact on the lives of ATG members varies according to the individual, but many people particularly emphasise that their level of confidence and sensitivity vis-à-vis things which occur in society has grown markedly, and they are more ready to take up a clearly-defined position against injustices (e.g. by saying 'No'), as a result of the many years of honing vision and developing the capacity to intervene spontaneously. They also report that they have developed competencies which prove useful in their 'everyday' jobs; and over the years the links between these fields (e.g. in women's refuges, work with young people, in prisons and schools) and the work of ATG have been productively strengthened by regular meetings and the development of networks, e.g. between the public and private domains as well as between the professional and social.

THE HORIZON IS NOT THERE IN ORDER TO BE REACHED, BUT AS A GOAL TO STRIVE FOR

The group and the individual

A theatre group is enormously powerful; it can do much more than a single individual. At the same time, individuals have their own needs and capacities. The relationship needs continuous attention and negotiation. For instance, it is both inspiring and challenging to hear that Sanjoy Ganguly contributes all his workshop fee income to the group. Not everyone can do that, and each group has to find its own way to accommodate and nourish the individuals who make it up.

One key factor is agreement about goals. In its first two years ATG had a clear focus: to articulate opposition to extreme right-wing politics and to familiarise itself as much as possible with theatre practice. Here individual and common goals could be reconciled. It's important for members to recognise that they want both to develop as theatre practitioners and to pursue specific (political or social) goals. Then they can be clear about what the group means to them, how much they can contribute to it and what they can get out of it.

Over the years ATG has developed an extensive repertoire of issues (including for example joblessness, violence in the family, gender issues, as well as exploring the range and nature of political action). Another area of potential tension here is that between dramaturgy/theatre aesthetics and political aims. One challenge for the future may be to stimulate debate on a local or national scale by looking in depth at a particular issue.

Figure 68 ATG-Halle and Jana Sanskriti, Muktadhara IV Festival 2010

Figure 69 Ecumenical Christmas, Jana Sanskriti 2010

Making contact and working together with Jana Sanskriti in India has built up gradually, step by step, over the years. At the beginning it was just a few members of ATG who went to India and came back full of enthusiasm to tell the rest in Halle about it. From 2009, when the core team from Jana Sanskriti came to Halle after the Festival in Austria, real insight into each others' living and working conditions began to develop along with a much better sense of how these related to each other. At the very least everyone could get a feeling for what life was like, even if they couldn't understand all of it. The Indian agricultural workers came into contact with punks and hippies, the squats, Berlin and Halle; the ATG members experienced the metropolis of Kolkata and the villages of the Ganges delta.

What did these meetings set in motion? The gradual acquaintance with other ways of life and then bringing that back as a group into one's own sphere of action, working through culture shock and what results from it, all this will only fully reveal itself with time. At any rate for the group it acted as a stimulus to

281

start to come to terms with issues of global inequality, the North-South problematic and the ensuing political debates. Lots of things were the exact opposite of what people were used to at home, but they seemed to work. Traffic for example. Absolutely disciplined in Germany, total chaos in Kolkata. The attitude to time, different ways of keeping appointments and planning. But living side by side worked. So there is more than one way of doing things. And if Jana Sanskriti hadn't come to Germany, some members of ATG would never have gone to India. Direct face-to-face meeting with people is so important; more important than anything in books.

And India displayed, nakedly and in-your-face, things we've learned to cover up in Europe. For example the oppression of women. And yet in India the remark that the situation of women is really shocking gets the response 'And what about in your country? Is it really different there?' You have to look again at your own reality and admit that no, it's not all that different, just a bit less obvious. Men get paid more, women have to pay higher health insurance, and so on. Not all men are dinosaurs, many things have just become part of the accepted way of behaving for women and they have to liberate themselves from them all over again. Bárbara Santos's Madalena workshops provide an experimental play-space and a laboratory for doing that. In my own theatre group moments like this give rise to introspection which results in a confession: here too, women spend more time in the kitchen and do more tidying up and consequently they are often missing when decisions are made. Cleaning up tires you out, you can't fully take part in the discussion.

So the gifts of intercultural meetings – some welcome, some difficult to accept – are that things that were hidden become visible; and that's a chance to change them.

The meaning of the Indian experience for theatre aesthetics

Forum Theatre and the working processes which underpin it sometimes don't get the attention they need in terms of continuous evaluation of working practice. The aesthetics of Jana Sanskriti's work, the sense of joy they bring to the work and its energy and vitality, which stands out in their plays in spite of the often grim themes, was a real inspiration for ATG Halle.

The lively effect was made up of many things: putting together a repertoire of songs they can sing at any time and making it their own; incorporating a south-Indian stick-dance which can also be taught to children; creating a dramaturgy which uses circle forms, songs and powerful images, intermingled with dialogic scenes. Further, incorporating mythological forms and religious elements, linking current political situations with the narrative of the community. All these aesthetic elements communicate through the whole spectrum of sensory and sense-making channels and *Forum Theatre* takes on a significant creative dimension, which offers lots of dynamic possibilities for subsequently working out suggested solutions offered by spectactors.

(The above section is based on discussions with members[109] of ATG Halle which took place in December 2010 on the roof of Jana Sanskriti's office in Badu, Kolkata.)

....

109 Anke Zimpel, Kathryn Lau, Olaf Brand and Peter Igelmund.

Further considerations for working with theatre groups – a few useful questions to ask

The section on ATG Halle makes clear how many things there are to consider in relation to life in a theatre group. Here are a few questions to ponder. Use them as an inspiration and don't feel pressurised by them!

On plays

How is the process of constructing the plays tackled? What kind of 'politics' are involved? Is there an author? Or is the work truly collective (involving the group, the director and the public)? How complex is the presentation and analysis of the conflict in question?

What aesthetic strategies are employed (suspense, links between scenes, time-and-space-markers, alienation effects etc.)?

How does the play use music, colours, costumes, lighting? How does it adapt to the performance space? Does it speak to the community's collective memory?

How far is it possible, in the play and in the work towards it, to 'shake up' dominant cultural assumptions, to bring them into question? Does it address the way controlling myths operate in society?

Figure 70 *TO Vienna*, Creación Colectiva with Carlos Zatizabal 2009

Figure 71 *TO Vienna*, Creación Colectiva with Carlos Zatizabal 2009

On the work of actors as (Art)activists

Does the group have links to other political or cultural organisations? How does it go about relating to the public? Does it build up a regular audience which supports it and shares its intellectual journey?

How does it work with the audience during performances? Is the public invited to be a part of the rehearsal process? Does the group go on tour in order to enter into discussion with new audiences?

On work in the Group

Who leads workshops?

What kind of training does the group use for its work on acting?

What more advanced TO methods is it familiar with and using?

Do all group members receive training as Jokers or Multipliers?

How?

Does the group participate in festivals?

Summary: Themes Part D

Transcultural action and thought in a world-wide community of theatre activists; passing on the flame; TO as a feminist and emancipatory theatre movement; positioning one's own work in the global spectrum; art as a peaceful means and path to the democratisation of society; the experiment of communal living; political reflections on one's own career choices.

The end. Finish. It's never finished.

Appendix 1 – A story on the theme of collective anxiety and courage

Contributed by Hector Aristizábal

The Tale of Nebuyenga

Once upon a time there was a village in Africa and the people thought they had a community until one day a monster appeared.

The monster had legs as big as tree trunks and its mouth was a cave. When it pissed, poison wells would appear; when it drank, rivers would empty. No one knew where the monster came from. Some said it had been here when the Earth was still cooling. Others said it came from the forest where it had been abandoned by its mother and grown up full of rage. Whatever the reason, the monster showed up at the crossroads and began demanding food and people started giving it what it wanted.

It got so that Nebuyenga got fat off the food and grew larger and larger, ever more fearsome. And this went on for many years. Then, one summer, there was a drought. This was serious and the elders got together and met. Since there was less food it was decided that Nebuyenga would have to get less as well. A delegation was sent to the crossroads to tell the monster the news. But Nebuyenga looked at the small amount of food that was sent and became enraged. He devoured the food, ate the cups and plates and then in his rage and hunger, he wildly reached out and ripped the arm off one of the youths who had come with the wagon of food.

Nebuyenga liked the taste of what he had eaten.

'Bring me more of that!' he shouted. 'That's what I like.'

The elders met again after that and discussed what was being asked of them. Some wanted to kill the monster right then and there. But many in the village were afraid of Nebuyenga. So they gave him what he wanted, a youth every week, selected from the slaves.

This went on for some time until only one youth was left in the village, the chief elder's son. When his turn came to be sacrificed, he screamed out in horror. 'I'll kill the monster myself.' But the women of the village had already made a decision. They had used their knowledge of the herbs and plants to make a huge bowl of poison that would trick Nebuyenga.

That afternoon, they bought the concoction out to the crossroads. Nebuyenga drank it in one gulp and demanded to know where the sacrificial youth was. There was nothing but silence and Nebuyenga flew into a rage. In his ravenous hunger, he started eating himself. First he ate his arms, then his thighs, then his torso and then his head. Soon they only thing left was his stomach. That's when the rain started pelting the Earth. It rained for 20 days and 20 nights. Finally the stomach melted into the Earth.

People came from the village and started to dance on the ground where Nebuyenga had consumed himself. But even as they did they heard a voice. 'Don't you know I'm always hungry?' For the truth is Nebuyenga is everywhere. He lives in any community that puts up with him. And his favourite smell is fear.

Appendix 2 – Story on the theme of Initiation into society and into one's own life

Contributed by Hector Aristizábal

The Half Boy

Once upon a time there was a village and in that village a boy was born. It happened that when the boy was born it was only half of the boy that came out. And in this case it was only the left side, meaning the left side of the head, the left arm, the left side of the torso, the left leg. As far as the right side went, it was a complete omission, nothing was there whatsoever.

As you can imagine, when the boy realised that he was going to be thrust into life as only half of what he wanted to be and half of what everyone else expected to see, he didn't feel very happy. Actually he started lamenting about his condition and he directed his lament mostly toward those close to him, which turned out to be mostly his family.

As the half boy grew – because even a half boy can grow – he became more vociferous about his laments and soon they reached beyond his parent's hut and into the huts of neighbours and soon permeated the entire village.

When the boy became what we now call an adolescent, he decided to leave the village. To tell you the truth the people from the village didn't try to stop him and on the contrary they were happy to see him depart. The half boy left the village the way a half boy moves. The half boy went on for a short while or a long while – the story doesn't say – until he was far from his village.

He finally arrived at the bank of a river and there he sat on top of a rock and continued his laments. He lamented against his condition, against his family, against his village, against life itself, against God. He was vociferously doing so when all of a sudden he noticed someone coming towards him. He discovered that it was another half boy and this half was the right side. Without thinking the half boy found himself moving toward the other half boy and soon they found themselves facing each other...

What do you think happened?

The two boys started wrestling and their encounter was so intense that soon in the place of their struggle a cloud of dust was all that could be seen. After a while, the cloud of dust fell into the nearby river and disappeared, creating great commotion in the waters; minutes later even the bubbles subsided and then, after an even longer while...

A full boy came out of the water, terribly confused, not knowing who he was, not knowing where he was, not knowing whether to put the right foot or the left foot first. Somehow he managed to start moving and did so for a while – a long while or a short while, the story doesn't say – until the full boy arrived at the outskirts of a village where an elder was standing. The boy approached the elder and asked him: 'Excuse me, could you please tell me where I am, I am lost and don't know where to go.' The elder looked at the boy and said: 'You are back at the very place where you started from and now because you are back and only because you are back will we be able to celebrate'. A great cele-bration was immediately prepared, all kinds of delicious foods were brought, drumming, dancing and singing took place; and a group of young people told this exact story to a group of inhabitants of the village.

Appendix 3 – International Theatre of the Oppressed Organisation (ITO) – Declaration of principles

Preamble

1. The basic aim of the Theatre of the Oppressed is to humanise Humanity.
2. The **Theatre of the Oppressed** is a system of Exercises, Games and Techniques based on *Essential Theatre*, to help men and women to develop what they already have inside themselves: theatre.

Essential Theatre

3. Every human being is theatre!
4. Theatre is defined as the simultaneous existence – in the same space and context – of actors and spectators. Every human being is capable of seeing the situation and seeing him/herself in the situation.
5. Essential theatre consists of three elements: Subjective Theatre, Objective Theatre and Theatrical Language
6. Every human being is capable of acting: to survive, we necessarily have to produce actions and observe those actions and their effects on the environment. To be Human is to be Theatre: the co-existence of actor and spectator in the same individual. This is *Subjective Theatre*.
7. When human beings limit themselves to observing an object, a person or a space, momentarily renouncing their capacity and necessity of acting, the energy and desire to act is transferred to that space, person or object, creating a space inside a space: an Aesthetic Space. This is *Objective Theatre.*
8. All human beings use, in their daily lives, the same language that actors use on the stage: their voices, their bodies, their movements and their expressions; they translate their emotions and desires into *Theatrical Language.*

Theatre of the Oppressed

9. The Theatre of the Oppressed offers everyone the aesthetic means to analyse their past, in the context of their present, and subsequently to invent their future, without waiting for it. The Theatre of the Oppressed helps human beings to recover a language they already possess – we learn how to live in society by playing theatre. We learn how to feel by feeling; how to think by thinking; how to act by acting. Theatre of the Oppressed is rehearsal for reality.

10. The *Oppressed* are those individuals or groups who are socially, culturally, politically, economically, racially, sexually, or in any other way deprived of their right to *Dialogue* or in any way impaired to exercise this right.

11. *Dialogue* is defined as to freely exchange with others, as a person and as a group, to participate in human society as equal, to respect differences and to be respected.

12. The Theatre of the Oppressed is based upon the principle that all human relationships should be of a dialogic nature: among men and women, races, families, groups and nations, dialogue should prevail. In reality, all dialogues have the tendency to become monologues, which creates the *Oppressor – Oppressed* relationship. Acknowledging this reality, the main principle of Theatre of the Oppressed is to help restoring dialogue among human beings.

Principles and Objectives

13. The Theatre of the Oppressed is a worldwide non-violent aesthetic movement which seeks for peace, not passivity.

14. The Theatre of the Oppressed tries to activate people in a humanistic endeavour expressed by its very name: *theatre of, by, and for the op-*

pressed. A system that enables people to act in the fiction of theatre to become protagonists, i.e. acting subjects, of their own lives.

15. The Theatre of the Oppressed is neither an ideology nor a political party, neither dogmatic nor coercive and is respectful of all cultures. It is a method of analysis and a means to develop happier societies. Because of its humanistic and democratic nature, it is widely used all over the world, in all fields of social activities such as: education, culture, arts, politics, social work, psychotherapy, literacy programmes and health.

16. Theatre of the Oppressed is now being used in dozens of nations around the world, as a tool for the making of discoveries about oneself and about the Other, of clarifying and expressing our desires; a tool for the changing of circumstances which produce unhappiness and pain and for the enhancement of what brings peace; for respecting differences between individuals and groups and for the inclusion of all human beings in Dialogue; and finally a tool for the achievement of economic and social justice, which is the foundation of true democracy. Summarising, the general objective of the Theatre of the Oppressed is the development of essential Human Rights.

The International *Theatre of the Oppressed* Organization (ITO)

17. The ITO is an organization that coordinates and enhances the development of Theatre of the Oppressed all over the world, according to the principles and objectives of this Declaration.

18. The ITO does so by connecting Theatre of the Oppressed practitioners into a global network, fostering exchange and methodological development; by facilitating training and multiplication of the existing techniques; by conceiving projects on a global scale; by inspiring the creation of local *Centres for Theatre of the Oppressed* (CTO's); by promoting and creating conditions for the work of CTO's and practitioners and by creating an international meeting point on the internet.

19. The ITO is of the same humanistic and democratic nature as its principles and objectives; it will incorporate any contributions from those who are working under this Declaration of Principles.
20. The ITO will assume that anyone using the various techniques of Theatre of the Oppressed subscribes to this Declaration of Principles.

Appendix 4 – The Stories of Virgílio and the Fat Lady

Freely adapted from Augusto Boal

Like Paulo Freire, Augusto Boal was an inspiring teacher who often taught through stories. He had a wonderful way of recollecting experiences so that their meaning could become clear without ever losing vitality. He was able to transmit epiphanies and moments when his life changed as a result of a profound insight, in such a way that the epiphany could be shared by others and he could take his audience on a journey.

Virgílio

As the political situation in Brazil at the beginning of the 1960s became more and more tense, artists could no longer put up with it. They tried to fulfil their mission as artists within society and went on tour. Augusto Boal took his theatre company to the north-east of the country and presented a play which ended in the following way:

All the actors were standing on the stage with a rifle in one hand and a flag in the other. They sang in harmony 'We'll spill our blood to save our land!' 'The land belongs to the people!' To every age there is an appropriate form of art. What they were offering was full-blooded propaganda theatre, as they understood it. The agricultural workers who made up the audience were very enthused. A man called Virgílio came up to Boal and congratulated him. He was astonished and moved that young people from the city should express solidarity with his community. And he said: 'Fantastic, you've come just at the right moment, we're going to have a celebration this evening. And tomorrow, can you see that house on the hill over there?' – and he pointed to it – 'Tomorrow we're going over there, that's where the landowner lives. Then we're going to burn the house down and chase him out.'

Boal and his actors and actresses became slightly nervous, he replied something like: 'Yes, OK, I'm very pleased that you liked the play. But hang on. These aren't real weapons that we're holding here, they're stage props.' And Virgílio replied: 'Ah, never mind, that's not a problem. We've got enough weapons for you.' Boal became even more nervous. And he said: 'Yes but, uh, listen: we really are actors, we're not agricultural workers. We've got to be in the next town tomorrow to perform the play again there.' Then Virgílio spoke the sentence that would change Augusto Boal's life: 'OK, I get it. So the blood that you want to spill, it's agricultural workers' blood, not actors' blood.' Augusto Boal and his actors and actresses felt immensely ashamed. To put it in Che Guevara's words: 'Solidarity means taking the same risk.' On stage they clearly didn't do that. The agricultural worker Virgílio, who had not had an education like Che Guevara, had immediately put his finger on the problem of political theatre at that time. Boal writes in his autobiography, *Hamlet and the Baker's Son*: 'From that moment on, my theatre changed. From that moment on it was no longer a theatre of answers but one of questions.'

That was the story of Virgílio, whom Augusto Boal would have very much liked to meet again in order to tell him how much this analysis had meant to him, but never got the chance.

The Fat Lady

A long time after Augusto Boal had gone over to showing problems on stage without offering solutions, the moment arrived which we nowadays think of as the birth of *Forum Theatre*. It took place in Peru, in a place called Chaclacayo.

In his autobiography Boal writes:

> Remembering today what I remembered yesterday, the thing remembered now differs from the memory before. Every day is a new day. I am no longer who I was only hours ago. My being is becoming. I never am: I am always becoming. I am that which I am not yet, and I am also what I have already ceased to be. In the act of approaching being, I become that which I shall never be, since, if I become by being it, I shall already be in transit to another being which I am not yet nor will be, as I am the first, always in transit. Inevitably.[110]

This results in the story being told as if most of it has been remembered (that's the way Augusto often told it), and a small part has been invented (coming from my imagination). There is no proof one way or the other.

A lady came to Augusto with a problem. She said: 'Augusto, I've heard you create theatre from stories about problems people have. I've got a problem. But I'll tell you straight out: it's not political. Can you help me with it?' Augusto replied: 'But Señora, all problems are political!' She contradicted him: 'Augusto, you've got it all wrong. My problem is – I've got a husband.' And Augusto was happy: 'Señora! In order to have a husband you have to have a registry office and a system of law and a state. You see! That's politics.' She did not agree with him, but she told him about her problem: for several months her husband had been going to the north every weekend to build a new house for them both. At the end of every week she gave him money for building materials, money that she had worked hard all week to earn.

The lady was illiterate. Eventually she began to be suspicious, this story about the house seemed to be going on forever, it couldn't possibly take that long. She demanded proof: 'Bring me the bills.' Then he brought her some coloured

110 Boal, Augusto, *Hamlet and the Baker's Son*, Routledge, London 2001, p. 206.

paper with writing on it that she couldn't decipher; and the whole thing gave off a scent of roses! She went to her neighbour: 'Read me what's written here. What's on these bills?' Her neighbour had to disappoint her: 'They aren't bills. They're love letters. From the woman your husband has been visiting for months every weekend with your money.' 'That's my situation.', said the lady to Augusto. 'Tomorrow evening he'll come home and I don't know what to do, because I know that in my situation divorce is not an option. If I separate from him, all the men in my village will think that I am theirs for the taking. For my own security I have to salvage this relationship. But this betrayal has got to cease. Augusto said: 'OK, I don't know what the solution is either, but we could make a play out of the story and then ask the audience. Perhaps they'll think of something.'

So now we get to the story within the story. The lady asked: 'You're making a play about my story? Can I come and watch?' For a moment Augusto was irritated, but then he thought: 'Well, OK, why not? What harm could it do?' Fortunately for us, he got it badly wrong at that moment! The rehearsal began. The actors came on to the stage, the cast was picked. The woman who up until this point had been sitting quietly in the auditorium, broke in: 'Augusto, who is this man?' Augusto answered in a slightly annoyed way: 'Señora, that's your husband.' 'What???' she shot back at him. 'You really think in all seriousness that I'd marry someone like that?' It went on like that, she found fault with everything until Augusto impatiently cried out: 'Señora if you can do it better, OK, come up here and take over my job!' He was certain that you had to have a proper director and that she would ask for his help within ten minutes at the most. Well, that wasn't how it was. She directed the scene without a problem, she was the expert on her own experience. And Augusto understood: everybody can be a director, not just Directors. That was the first important occurrence of that day. The evening arrived, the public came, the scene was performed up until the moment when the husband came back and knocked on the door. At that moment the play was stopped and Augusto asked the audience to help: 'What should the woman do now? What could she do?' The audience had many suggestions. Some people thought she should cry. She should cry desperately and then she should forgive her husband, because after all she wanted to keep him. So the actors began the scene from the beginning again. The husband knocked at the door, the wife opened it to him and wept and wept and wept. And then she said: 'You pig! I know everything! It's got to stop! And now I forgive you!' and the husband took his shoes off, sat down on the sofa, put his feet on the table and turned the TV on: 'Good', he said, 'now go in the kitchen and bring my dinner.'

The audience wasn't at all satisfied. The wife wasn't satisfied. Augusto wasn't satisfied. What else could be done? What other ideas were there?

In the back row of the theatre there was a fat lady. She was tremendously large. And furious. She was red in the face with anger. She was frowning. She was breathing heavily. Augusto asked: 'Señora, I have the impression that you've got an idea?' *Do* I have an idea!', came the answer. 'Then tell us what it is please', Augusto invited her. 'The wife should speak very clearly with her husband', she demanded. Augusto was disappointed. He had expected something a bit more dramatic. But OK. The actors went on stage, the husband knocked at the door, the wife opened: 'Clearly I know everything now. It's clear that all this has got to stop. It's very clear that you're a pig. And clearly I forgive you'. The husband took his shoes off, sat on the sofa, put his legs on the table, and turned the TV on. 'Good. And clearly it's now time you went into the kitchen to get my dinner.' Everyone was completely disappointed. The lady in the back row of the theatre was now so furious that she was practically levitating with anger. She began to leave the theatre. Now *that* was something that Augusto found very hard to take. He approached her cautiously. Standing before her, he said in a gentle voice: 'Señora, I've got the impression you're not very happy. I have the feeling that our actors are too stupid to understand you. Why don't you come on stage and show us what you mean by: 'She should speak clearly to him?'; and he looked at her quizzically.

And the lady changed on the spot. She became friendly and even somewhat embarrassed and shy. She was as excited as a young deer. 'What me? On stage? May I really do that?'; and Augusto said: 'Yes, naturally.'

Then she got up. And the stage floor shook. The walls vibrated. Beads of sweat gathered on the forehead of the actor who was playing the husband. In a trembling voice he asked Augusto: 'Augusto, Augusto, what should I do now?' Augusto answered, very much a director of his time: 'Think of Stanislavski. Do everything just as you've learned.'

The lady climbed the steps to the stage. She walked up the actor playing the husband. She got him in a headlock with one arm. With the other she grabbed the broomstick. And she beat him mercilessly, without saying a word. Then she dropped both the broom and the husband. She went to the sofa. Sat down. Put her feet on the table, turned the TV on and said: 'And now. YOU go in the kitchen and bring me my dinner!'

At that moment *Forum Theatre* was born, and its first rule was: no physical violence on stage! If there is a need to use violence, then do it this way: in slow motion; with a time limit; and keep two metres distance between the participants.

We don't know what happened to the actor who played the husband. Augusto just thought that after this experience he would certainly never, for the rest of his life, get the idea of going behind his wife's back. The motto that *Theatre of the Oppressed* derived from this intervention was: 'Don't say what you're thinking, show us what you mean.' And that is true even today. So that's the story of the birth of *Forum Theatre*.

Bibliography

By Augusto Boal

BOAL, Augusto, *Theatre of the Oppressed*, Pluto Classics, London 1998.

BOAL, Augusto, *Games for Actors and Non-Actors*, Routledge, London 1998.

BOAL, Augusto, *Juegos para actores y no actores*, Alba Editorial, Barcelona 2001.

BOAL, Augusto, *The Rainbow of Desire, The Boal Method of Theatre and Therapy*, Routledge, London 1998.

BOAL, Augusto, *El arco iris del deseo, del teatro experimental a la terapia*, Alba Editorial, Barcelona 2004.

BOAL, Augusto, *Legislative Theatre*, Routledge, London 1998.

BOAL, Augusto, *Hamlet and the Baker's Son*, Routledge, London 2001.

BOAL, Augusto, *O teatro como arte marcial,* Editora Garamond, Rio de Janeiro 2003.

BOAL, Augusto, *The Aesthetics of the Oppressed*, Routledge, London 2006.

BOAL, Augusto, *A Estética do Oprimido*, Garamond, Rio de Janeiro 2009.

BOAL, Augusto, GUARNIERI, Gianfrancesco, 'Arena cuenta Zumbi', in: *Primer Acto, Brasil: Teatro de la Represion*, Número 146 – 147, Madrid 1972.

BOAL, Augusto, 'Torquemada', Henschelverlag, Berlin 1975, unpublished manuscript.

BOAL, Augusto, *Técnicas latinoamericanas de teatro popular (Una revolución copernicana al revés)*, Corregidor, Buenos Aires 1975.

BOAL, Augusto, *A deliciosa e sangrenta aventura latina de jane spitfire, espiã e mulher sensual!*, Moræs Editores, Lissabon 1977.

By Julian Boal

BOAL, Julian, *Imagens de um teatro popular*, Hucitec, Sao Paulo 2000.

By Paulo Freire

FREIRE, Paulo, *Pedagogy of the Oppressed*, Continuum, London & New York 2000.

FREIRE, Paulo, *Education, the Practice of Freedom*, Writers' and Readers' Publishing Co-operative, London 1973.

FREIRE, Paulo, *Pedagogy of Hope*, Continuum, London & New York 2004.

Secondary Literature on the *Theatre of the Oppressed*

BABBAGE, Frances, *Augusto Boal*, Routledge, London & New York 2004.

SCHUTZMAN, Mady & COHEN CRUZ, Jan (Eds.), *Playing Boal, Theatre, Therapy, Activism*, Routledge, London & New York 1994.

SCHUTZMAN, Mady & COHEN CRUZ, Jan (Eds.), *A Boal Companion, Dialogues on Theatre and Cultural Politics*, Routledge, New York 2006.

Publications by and about individuals and groups, who work with *Theatre of the Oppressed*

GANGULY, Sanjoy, *Where we Stand, Five Plays of the Repertoire of Jana Sanskriti*, CAMP, Kolkata 2009.

GANGULY, Sanjoy, *Jana Sanskriti, Forum Theatre and Democracy in India*, Routledge, London & New York 2010.

DA COSTA, Dia, (Ed.), *Scripting Power: Jana Sanskriti On and Offstage*, CAMP, Kolkata 2010.

ARISTIZÁBAL, Hector & LEFER, Diane, *The Blessing next to the Wound, A Story of Arts, Activism, and Transformation*, Lantern Books, New York 2010.

DIAMOND, David, *Theatre for Living, The Art and Science of Community – based Dialogue*, Trafford Publishing, Victoria 2007.

Journals

Centro de Teatro do Oprimido (Eds.), *Metaxis*, Nos. 1 – 6 (2001 – 2010).

Contemporary Theatre Review, an international Journal, Volume 3, Part 1 (1995): 'Working Without Boal: Digressions and Developments in the Theatre of the Oppressed', Harwood Academic Publishers.

Practical Handbooks for Theatre work

BAIM, Clark, BROOKES, Sally & MOUNTFORD, Alun, *The Geese Theatre Handbook: Theatre with Offenders and People at Risk*, Waterside Press, Winchester 2002.

BARKER, Clive, *Theatre Games: A New Approach to Drama Training*, Methuen Drama, London 1977

CALLERY, Dymphna, *Through the Body: A Practical Guide to Physical Theatre*, Nick Hern Books, London 2001

JOHNSTON, Chris, *House of Games: Making Theatre from Everyday Life*, Routledge, London 1998.

JOHNSTONE, Keith, *Impro: Improvisation and the Theatre*, Faber, London 1979.

JOHNSTONE, Keith, *Impro for Storytellers: theatresports and the art of making things happen*, Faber, London 1999.

MARTIN, John, *The Intercultural Performance Handbook*, Routledge, London 2004.

SPOLIN, Viola, *Improvisation for the theatre: a handbook of teaching and directing techniques*, Pitman, London 1973.

THOMPSON, James, *Drama Workshops for Anger Management and Offending Behaviour*, Jessica Kingsley Publishers, London & Philadelphia 1999.

THOMPSON, James (Ed.), *Prison Theatre, Perspectives and Practices*, Jessica Kingsley Publishers, London & New York 1998.

Secondary Literature on Theatre

BOON, Richard and PLASTOW, Jane, *Theatre and Empowerment: Community Drama on the World Stage*, CUP, Cambridge 2004

TURNER, Victor, *From Ritual to Theatre*, Performing Arts Journal Publications, 1982.

VAN ERVEN, Eugène, *Community Theatre: Global Perspectives,* Routledge, London 2000.

On Somatic Learning and Body Work

BERINGER, Elizabeth (Ed.), *Embodied Wisdom, The Collected Papers of Moshé Feldenkrais*, North Atlantic Books, Berkeley 2010

FELDENKRAIS, Moshé, *Awareness through Movement*, Arkana, London 1990

FELDENKRAIS, Moshé, *The Elusive Obvious*, Meta Publications, Cupertino, CA 1981.

FELDENKRAIS, Moshé, *The Potent Self*, Harper & Row Publishers, San Francisco & New York 1993

On perception

MATURANA, Humberto & VARELA, Francisco, *The Tree of Knowledge: the biological roots of human understanding*, Shambhala Publications, Boston 1987

On Latin America

GALEANO, Eduardo, *Open Veins of Latin America: five centuries of the pillage of a continent*, Monthly Review Press, New York 1997

On manipulation in comics

DORFMAN, Ariel, *The Empire's Old Clothes: What the Lone Ranger, Babar, and Other Innocent Heroes, do to our minds*, Durham, Duke University Press, North Carolina 1983

On Fals Borda and Participatory Action Research

REASON, Peter & BRADBURY, Hilary (Eds.), *Handbook of Action Research, Participative Inquiry and Practice*, Sage Publications, London 2001

GREENWOOD, J. Davydd & LEVIN, Morten, *Introduction to action research: Social research for social change*, Sage Publications, London 1998

Websites of the *Theatre of the Oppressed*

www.theatreoftheoppressed.org

This is the website which Formaat has for years made available to the International Community. We hope it will continue to be a resource for useful material. Alternatives are being developed at present.

Many people and groups in the Community are on Facebook and there is a new initiative, ToPnewmedia Forum. The host is Uri Noy-Meir.

Here I list a few representative groups on different continents; contact with others may be obtained through them.

The website of CTO Rio: www.cto.org.br

The Theatre and Pedagogy of the Oppressed Conference: www.ptoweb.org

Augusto Boal Archive and Blog of Instituto Boal:
http://institutoaugustoboal.wordpress.com/author/institutoaugustoboal/

Bárbara Santos, Brazil & Germany:
http://kuringa-barbarasantos.blogspot.co.at

Chen Alon, Combatants for Peace, Israel/Palestine: www.cfpeace.org

Adrian Jackson, London. Cardboard Citizens. Theatre with and for the homeless: www.cardboardcitizens.org.uk

Geraldine Ling, Newcastle-upon-Tyne. The Lawnmowers. TO group with and for people with learning difficulties: www.thelawnmowers.co.uk

Tim Wheeler, Bradford. Mind the Gap. TO group with and for people with learning difficulties: www.mindthegaptheatre.com

New York: www.toplab.org

Mariana Villani, Argentina: teatreviesas.blogspot.com

Senegalese *Theatre of the Oppressed* movement: www.kadduyaraax.com

Singapore: www.dramabox.org

Xris Reardon, Australia: www.thirdwaytheatre.org

Agneta Josephson, Breyta. Swedish TO group:
forumtheaternbreyta@gmail.com

Muriel Naessens, French Network. Le Féminisme Enjeux:
http://feminisme-enjeux-theatre-opprime.overblog.com

Group und Network Platform *Theatre of the Oppressed – Vienna*:
www.tdu-wien.at

Birgit Fritz / Abel Solares, Austria. Site for exploratory theatre work and somatic learning: www.inexactart.com

Credits for Images and Photographs

Agneta Josephson:	Fig. 47
Alina Serban/Oliver Gross:	Figs. 25, 27, 70, 71
ArtamugarriaK/Alex Carrascosa:	Figs. 61, 62
Barbara Palffy:	Figs. 54, 55, 56, 57
Birgit Fritz:	Figs. 1, 13, 14, 26, 28, 29, 34, 60, 63, 69, Cover Image
Isabel Maria Valentim Leal:	Figs. 40, 41, 42
Karl Koschek:	Figs. 2, 3, 4, 7, 9, 10, 11, 12, 16, 17, 18, 19, 20, 21, 22, 23, 24, 30, 31, 32, 33, 35, 36, 51, 52, 53, 58, 64, 65, 66, 67, 68
Matthias Thonhauser:	Figs. 5, 46
Sonja Katzmayer:	Figs. 37, 38
Susanne Kreuzberger:	Figs. 44, 45
TO Vienna, archive material:	Figs. 6, 8, 15, 39, 43, 48, 49, 50, 59

Glossary

TO   *Theatre of the Oppressed*

ITO   International *Theatre of the Oppressed* Organisation

ATO   Association of *Theatre of the Oppressed*

CTO   Centre of *Theatre of the Oppressed*

GTO   Group of *Theatre of the Oppressed*

Arsenal of the *Theatre of the Oppressed*: Augusto Boal's term for the collected techniques of the *Theatre of the Oppressed*

Tree of the *Theatre of the Oppressed*: diagrammatic representation of the organic nature of the techniques of the *Theatre of the Oppressed*

Madalena: Feminist wing of the *Theatre of the Oppressed*, women-only workshops

Joker: Moderator of a *Forum Theatre* play

The following are terms used at CTO Rio:

Community Joker: Jokers who work with local TO groups as trainers and facilitators and may moderate their *Forum Theatre* plays.

Multiplying Joker/Kuringa: Jokers who make possible the multiplication and cascading of methods and techniques of TO. For this they need to possess a profound knowledge of the practice and theory, be firmly established within the International Community and possess a global perspective.

Assistant Joker: on the way to becoming independent Jokers, they accompany experienced Jokers in their work and take charge of some aspects of the process: they are doing a kind of 'job-shadowing'.

Under Pressure	Internet-Publication of the ITO (available as an archive)
Metaxis	Specialist Journal of CTO Rio
TO Laboratory	*Theatre of the Oppressed* Laboratory
Creación Colectiva	Process of collective creation of plays
Teatro Popular	People's Theatre

Information about the people who have contributed to the book

Ralph Yarrow

Ralph Yarrow is a teacher, director and actor. He started the MA in Theatre and Development at UEA, Norwich, UK and has worked for many years with Jana Sanskriti in West Bengal, as well as with other groups in India. He has written books on improvisation and Indian theatre, and has worked as a director in both English and French, in Great Britain, India and South Africa.

Julian Boal

Co-founder and member of GTO-Paris and Féminisme – Enjeux, internationally active, freelance workshop leader (for example in Brazil, India, Switzerland, Bosnia, Croatia, Italy, Spain, Austria, Kyrgyzstan, and the USA), author of 'Imagens de um teatro popular, Huitec, 2000', translator of *The Rainbow of Desire* into French, worked for many years with his father. Supports TO groups around the world in their development and training.

Contact: julian.boal@gmail.com

Sanjoy Ganguly

Sanjoy Ganguly is a maker of socio-political theatre and founder of the theatre group network Jana Sanskriti, which is active in twelve Indian states and has over one thousand members. Those involved are farmers, women, untouchables, slum residents, Hindus and Muslims, who have found in the medium of theatre, a method with which to discuss their problems and improve their situation.

Sanjoy Ganguly teaches as a guest lecturer at international universities, for example, in Canada and the UK and is a regular guest of the British Council in the fields of theatre, development and social change.

www.janasanskriti.org

Bárbara Santos

Coordinator of the Centro de Teatro do Oprimido – Rio from 1994 – 2008, leads and plans TO projects for communities, schools, culture centres, hospitals and prisons, she spreads the methods of the *Theatre of the Oppressed* worldwide. She is a woman, black, mother, South American, Brazilian, sociologist, actor and Kuringa. Her international experience has led her to, among other places, Guinea-Bissau, Mozambique, Angola, Senegal, Canada, Palestine, Egypt, Hong Kong, Croatia, Germany and Austria. She supervises, leads and accompanies TO groups around the world.

kuringa-bárbarasantos.blogspot.com

rio-berlim-rio.blogspot.com

ctorio.org.br

Hector Aristizábal

Born and grew up in Medellin, Columbia; trained as an actor and psychologist, he uses both acting and therapy as well as activism to create theatre, animating imagination and taking a stance towards the world and its condition.

In his solo piece, 'Nightwind', he tell his own story of imprisonment and torture in 1982, by the US supported Columbian military. He is cofounder of ImagineAction, a multidisciplinary group specialised on creating dialogue with communes, social justice and transformation. Through workshops, performances and other creative events, ImaginAction invites us to explore embodied knowledge, reactivating and incorporating the creativity of all people to build a more just and joyful quality of life.

Imaginaction.org

www.soaw.org

Lana Sendzimir

Grew up in both Europe and the USA, moving in between languages and cultures – and is still searching for her roots. She studied *Theatre and Media for Development* in the UK before going on to train with Birgit Fritz in Vienna from 2010 – 2011, as well as with other practitioners, like Hector Aristizábal, Bárbara Santos, and Ronald Matthijssen. She was part of the Austrian *Pioneers of Change 2012* and is co-founder and facilitator at *actinGreen*, a theatre group working to inspire environmental consciousness and action through creative processes, bringing together the arts, experiential education and a love for nature, with the aim to reconnect people to the(ir) environment, both inside and out. She currently works as a workshop leader and teacher in Austria.

www.actingreen.at

www.pioneersofchange.at

Thanks

Thanks to Augusto Boal, who helped me through challenging times and enabled me to find my own way in life inspired by his life's work, his resourceful generosity, his apparently endless trust and his love for human beings.

Thanks to Ronald Matthijssen, who was the first person prepared to share his capacities with me and Luc Opdebeeck, who together with Ronald invited me to Rotterdam a long time ago.

Thanks to Julian Boal, who spontaneously came to Vienna to help us start our first *Forum Theatre* group.

Thanks to Dietlind Schwarzenberger, who trusted me with her work. This trust changed my life.

To Gerhard Bisovsky, who opens doors. To Wolfgang Dietrich, who widens horizons. To Marietta Schneider, who accompanies and supports. To Franz Nest, who appeared at the right moment.

And thanks to all the players who were prepared to embark on this adventure and many other adventures! Thanks to Christoph Seidl, Sonja Katzmayer, Margit Schwabe, Verena Hladik! To Ahmad Abu Kharma! To Osas Imafidon and Amas Adun! To Alina Serban! Angelique Lehmann! To Vera Rebl! To Florian Jung!

Thanks to Sanjoy and Sima Ganguly and all the members of Jana Sanskriti, who brought a new, additional dimension to the work with the *Theatre of the Oppressed*, like working and living in a collective and the notion of belonging.

Thanks to Abel Solares, for his stories and wisdom, his years of support and friendship and solidarity.

And thanks

to Carlos Zatizabal, who brought us Creación Colectiva and much, much literature and history and theatre,

to Chen Alon, Iwan Brioc, Hector Aristizábal, Bárbara Santos,

to Agneta Josephson, Mariana Villana, Xris Reardon,

to Lisa Kolb-Mzalouet, the bridge builder of Austrian TO work between the centuries!

And to all the other artists and explorers, who brought and bring the various components of theatre work closer: Richard Nieoczym, Catherine Corray, Stephen Waugh, Eva Brenner, Marie Thérèse Escribano, Alex Carrascosa, Maria Nora, the WUK in Vienna and the many people who give the *Theatre of the Oppressed* a floor on which to stand, Johannes Benker, Wolfgang Schweiger, Irmgard Demirol, Renate Schneider, Werner Hörter, Vina Yun.

And to everyone who was there and moved on: among them – Twin Vision Theatre Group!

Special thanks to Zdravko Haderlap, who has generously opened his art-space 'a-zone' to us and to Karl Koschek, who with his dedication and patience for our work has made this publication possible.

Formatting and Graphics

DI Karl Koschek MBA
architecture, facility management
geomantic, csr management
&
photography
Vienna, Austria

contact: office@inexactart.com

ibidem-Verlag / *ibidem* Press
Melchiorstr. 15
70439 Stuttgart
Germany

ibidem@ibidem.eu
www.ibidem-verlag.com
www.ibidem.eu

CPSIA information can be obtained
at www.ICGtesting.com
Printed in the USA
LVOW13s1546010917
547251LV00011B/535/P